THE POWER OF
PRINCIPLED INCLUSION

THE POWER OF PRINCIPLED INCLUSION

How to be your best, most effective person in the world

MICHAEL G. SAWAYA

The Power of Principled Inclusion © Michael G. Sawaya, 2020

ISBN: 978-0-578-59790-4

Editing by Joan Dickson, Ph.D.
Cover and interior design by HR Hegnauer

1. Philosophy   2. Body, Mind, Spirit

The Observant Press
1600 Ogden Street
Denver, Colorado 80218
www.ObservantPress.com

AUTHOR'S NOTE

What a different world we are going to have when universally people are taught to be true to themselves, and operate from integrity with an understanding that each person is unique in their complexities. In this world each person will be encouraged to be powerful in their own sphere. People will be invited to bring their powerful selves to the interaction with others, emphasizing inclusivity and rejecting old notions that exclusivity is preferred. This book will set you on the path to finding that world, and you will be more powerful for it! The entire world will be better for it!

INTRODUCTION

My first book, *Turbulence in the River*, was a book about spirituality inspired by a series of unexpected events in my life that amounted to an almost four-year adventure in received teaching, and that taught me a great deal about reality, possibility, and the power of principled inclusion. Writing *Turbulence in the River* represented a truly personal journey that guided me forward along my spiritual path while opening me to my essential integrity. All that I have learned has been organized into four lessons: Gratitude, Calmness, Compassion, and Inclusion; and I was able to expand upon these two important truths: Love and Wisdom.

In my first book, I wrote about how I learned that Gratitude allows me to engage more meaningfully with the world, while Calmness teaches me how to disengage from turbulence. Building on these two principles, I discovered the depth of the meaning of Compassion, truly feeling both my own emotions and the emotions of others. I learned that Compassion is a prerequisite to finding one's own internal Inclusion. I learned that Inclusion is necessary for self-development and integrity. By practicing Inclusion, I came to understand how important it is to incorporate our entire being as part of the internal balance that we seek. As for Love, I now know that Love comes from the power of observation and that this power defines the essence of the creator. I learned, too, that Wisdom is the sum total of all the laws and rules that govern the infinite universe.

Turbulence in the River took its name from the conflict and discord that seems always to follow social interaction, as well as the turbulence we feel when trying to accommodate the disparate aspects of ourselves. Sometimes, it is our own inner conflicts that manifest turbulence, but just as often, turbulence results when we have internalized the attitudes and emotions of others. The struggle to find balance and integrity is a life-long chore, but also can be seen as a gift. In *Turbulence in the River,* I was able to explore the world and my place in it, deal with many conflicts known and unknown, and seek inclusion so that the disparate parts of myself were balanced. In doing so, I realized my own integrity. That's the gift.

Now, in 2019, spurred on by my concerns for five existential crises that fundamentally threaten our lives, our civilizations, and even the planet, in my new book, *The Power of Principled Inclusion*, I have advanced my ideas about inclusion to incorporate the world around us. I am convinced that it is only through understanding ourselves and embracing the world in which we live that we have any hope of meeting and overcoming the challenges that we face.

In *The Power of Principled Inclusion*, I write about the stark differences between inclusionary and exclusionary thinking especially as it exists in contemporary times, and the importance of opening ourselves to the world in order to find reasonable ways to include others. Our social methods, religions, social organizations and governments are based on exclusionary thinking and, therefore, built on some reasonable, but even more unreasonable ways to exclude rather than include others. Retreating to exclusionary thinking will not get us where we need to go. Exclusionary thinking will not bring us happiness. I am convinced that learning to be as inclusive as we reasonably can be is the goal we must all share.

Most people want to live more effective, comfortable, and well-balanced lives. Most people would like to be happy, and it seems obvious that some people are much happier than others. When we are comfortable with ourselves, it is easier to be comfortable with others. It is a powerful experience to lead and influence other people. Influence and leadership allow us to leverage our beliefs and opinions in the outside world, but that kind of power must start first with an internal balance, which starts by developing our interior lives.

At birth, our involvement with the world begins and continues for the rest of our lives. The manner and the quality of the interaction with the outer world depends greatly on how we develop our interior lives. When our interior lives are developed, we become well-balanced and self-aware making it much easier to influence others. For this reason, anyone interested in being more influential or moving more powerfully in the world should first, foremost, and always be interested in creating a balanced self with an emphasis on self-acceptance and self-development. Our interactions with the outer world are a part of a life-long process of self-awareness and self-development. By ignoring our interior lives, we live in peril of losing contact with both our true selves and the world around us.

Because each of our lives is composed of vast, intricate, and fascinating stories with many chapters and unforeseen endings, our connections, obligations, and responsibilities within the world around us are complicated. For all of us, there are hidden or obscure aspects that we prefer to keep that way. Our interior lives are not always "at home" with the rest of who we are or who we think we are. Most of us have shadow sides that we do not feel comfortable revealing or confronting even in private, and certainly, not in public. We may often be torn between different parts of ourselves or different and, sometimes, contradictory or competing, feelings and thoughts. It may be hard for any of us to feel motivated at all times or to know ourselves deeply and fully. Successful, internal integration requires a balance of thought, desires and emotional states. Successful living is an art, and finding the right balance in our lives is the work of a serious artist.

To fully bring who we are into the world is to experience the power of inclusion. Every leader in human history has had that power and a way to bring their personality into the outside world. To be sure, there are times that the leader needs to step back and figure out whether to interact, refrain from interacting, or disengage entirely. Truly, every leader must be a leader of themselves first before becoming a leader of others. In order to be forceful and influential, a leader must be able to muster all personal assets. Rarely, if ever, do leaders happen by accident. The assets and attributes that make them successful leaders do not spring up overnight, but are built over time, often after great internal struggle. The more interaction you have with the world, the more likely you will experience struggle, turmoil and turbulence. Anyone who seeks to be a leader or finds themselves in a leadership position should expect that additional interactions with others will bring their share of conflict. Whether you're a leader not, the ability to navigate turbulence internally and externally is a valuable skill that can be learned. By learning the skills of personal and internal inclusion, we are able to develop our thoughts, values, character, and beliefs. Development of fine-tuned principles aren't "givens" and don't just sprout automatically out of nowhere, but are always manifested in response to feedback, and may change over time as experience, curiosity, and a growing sense of discovery contribute to their development.

Some people have developed their principles to a much greater degree than others, and some are more comfortable with the principles and values that they have developed, but it is not unusual to feel ambivalent or conflicted about who we are and about our principles as well. It is common for anyone to feel that the past actions and thoughts of one day don't sit right with the next. We have all said and done things we wish we could undo if only we had found the foresight or fortitude to do so.

If you want to make a difference in the world, you must bring the force of your character, the focus of your thoughts, and the depth of your emotions to all encounters. You will need to be courageous. We can think about being courageous and that gets us ready for taking a stand on something, but there is always the added part of courage that requires us to be emotionally ready to take part in the action at hand. In doing so, we must recognize that we have to put our "heart into it" and, as the old expression goes: in Latin, the word for heart was "cor" and it came to the Old English language through the Old French word for heart also known as "corage". Although most folks have not given much thought about how to sense or feel their heart's location, it is possible to learn to do so.

When you have finished reading this book and studying the suggested methods, you will have the basis for finding your own internal congruence. That congruence should help you find your essential integrity. With that you can confidently interact with your community and your work in the most effective way

Balance, integrity, and self-awareness will help you develop, consciously or not, the principles that allow you to effectively confront your inner and outer world. The more you understand your personal principles, the easier it will be to apply them to the interactions that you have with everyone and everything in your life.

In a rapidly changing world, where older methods of employment have changed or been eliminated, and where the climate and biosphere is changing, our ability to bring our principles into the world has tremendous value. While it is true that luck may work for some, those people will not have the staying power that comes when one is truly aware of the internal principles that come with integrity.

Seldom does success and power come by accident, but, instead, a purposeful and focused intention based in courage and acting from that intention is called for. Hypocrisy will eventually fail, and a life without internal balance and self-awareness may end up being its own worst enemy. If powerful people were always successful and reasonably content, you would see less unhappiness and frantic activity. There would be much less exclusion among individuals, groups, and political entities, and, instead, we would likely find a universal veneration for all of life with the understanding that inclusion only strengthens and enriches each individual and our collective societal and cultural landscapes. In *The Power of Principled Inclusion*, we will explore the incentives and deep concerns that teach us why principled inclusion is vital for both personal effectiveness and the continued success of our human endeavors as well as the life around us.

WORKBOOK
Introduction

As a part of your encounter with your own powerful principles, this book includes a workbook at the end of each section so that you can write down your thoughts and reactions to the ideas and processes contained in each chapter. In preparation for this encounter, write down answers to the following:

1. What do you value most in the world and why?

2. Do you feel that what you value most in life is serving you?

3. What groups do you belong to (include employment, family and your circle of friends)?

4. Are you satisfied with your interaction with these groups?

5. Do you feel well served and embraced by the people around you?

6. Can you identify one main principle that you use for your interaction with those around you?

THE POWER OF
PRINCIPLED INCLUSION

1

THE FOUNDATION
OF ALL PRINCIPLES

Principles provide the structure for our lives,
but they cannot be sturdy or reliable
without a strong and deep foundation.

When we want to be reminded of how to see and enjoy the world, and how, perhaps, to be grateful, we should watch a child encounter it. The world is a fascinating place, and children cannot absorb it fast enough. Sometimes, it is also the case that children cannot discard it fast enough. Children are fascinated with everything new coming their way: a bug or a ball and anything else. All five senses must be satisfied and everything and anything explored. Children grow and develop by acting as if the world belongs to them, and may well show dissatisfaction if something is taken away before they're ready. It is not difficult to see how stunted a child would become if the world were not open for exploration. At some point, for most of us, the age of exploration, awe, and wonder comes to an end. Few of us can pinpoint when that happens, or exactly why it happens. We can only guess. Maybe it is because we started taking certain things for granted, started applying rules and world views we were taught whether they were true for us or not.

Unless we learn again how to explore and become more open to direct, authentic experiences, we cannot achieve personal importance. To the extent that anything is excluded from experience or contemplation, that part of the world will be limited. We can embrace things and exclude things as we go along, but we can't know what to embrace or exclude without, first, knowing something about it. When you know something well, you can trust your thoughts and feelings in regards to that something. When you really want to enjoy something, you will need to spend time experiencing it.

We cannot learn about, appreciate, or be grateful for something we have not, at least, observed. Observation and awareness are essential parts of all interaction. Sometimes, we need more than one of our senses to fully observe and to be fully aware. The more complicated something is, the more likely that understanding requires the involvement of multiple senses. Smell and taste, for example, often go together. We all know that touching and seeing are similarly compatible.

As we become more familiar with our surroundings, we might start taking them for granted and lose some of our sense of awareness. Once we have observed some *thing* a number of times, over some length of time, what we are observing can become stale, old, and even boring. Meaning may even be lost. By becoming aware that we are aware, we give ourselves the opportunity to reinvigorate the observation. By seeing it in a new light, we may find aspects that we had not previously observed, or that have changed in importance by becoming more or even less important, but at least no longer ignored. By sharpening our awareness and our ability to observe, we increase our ability to become part of our surroundings and to be grateful. Gratitude involves deep and respectful appreciation, which comes from the awareness of observation. It all starts with observation and culminates with a deep gratitude.

Our principles are derived from our values. Our values do not arise from a vacuum, but are inspired by the observations that come from interactions with the world. Some principles come from values taken on just as a child would without critical analysis. As the child grows into adulthood, these principles become habits much like a narrative that we have memorized.

When our values are working well for us, we enjoy the outer world with a sense of inner balance making critical analysis unnecessary. However, change is a constant, and to understand and to respond to our world from that understanding, we need to know what has changed, and how to accommodate the changes. Pretending that there has been no change is not being responsive. Acting as if change is wrong, and that all must return to the status quo, is also not being responsive, but rather merely reactive. There is no substitute for being observant or for looking at how we are being included in the world around us.

Like the gambler at the poker table, if we were simply machines looking to maximize our winnings, it might be easier to explain what happens as we encounter change. As far as we know, at this point in our evolution, human behavior, thinking, and emotion cannot be adequately explained by pure logic. You cannot always "think yourself into a state of happiness." It may be that happiness is not connected entirely to logic, but rather is always connected to, if not controlled by, emotion. Emotion may or may not connect to conscious thought, but there is no doubt that emotion is connected to the more intangible, less logical, and probably unconscious parts of ourselves. Since time immemorial, humans have understood that emotions are connected strongly to the heart. Heart awareness and consciousness is a valuable part of critical awareness, and is a vital part of how we truly feel. Having heart consciousness is important in knowing whether your values and principles are truly effective for all encounters.

Many artists, writers, thinkers, and philosophers have focused our attention on the importance of living in the Now as well as the importance of mindfulness. They remind us that we lose out when we don't bring our full sense of awareness to our surroundings. They tell us that we must be as present as we can to what we observe and feel.

A step beyond being in the Now is being aware that you are aware. Each one of us is different than who we were five, ten, or twenty years ago. Sometimes, things change quickly and, sometimes, things change slowly. Most people let life happen to them. They are in a reactive mode, often either resisting change, or simply allowing change to happen with little or no personal input.

Effective observation of ourselves requires awareness that we are aware. This is called a "meta-observation" or sensing and seeing from a distance.

Meta-observation always involves, at least, a bit of abstraction allowing us to find a new perspective. New levels of perception allow us to find new ways to conceptualize both ourselves and the outer world. With this kind of new observation and newly enhanced context, we can be much more effective in managing our internal selves. Practicing meta-observation can be easy for some and daunting for others. It is a subject worthy of deep study and practice. Suffice it to say, human awareness can have different levels, all of which allow deeper understanding of who we are and how we interact with life around us.

Principles are always personal in nature. You possess and are responsible for your principles. This is true even if your principles are adopted or adapted entirely from others. They are yours because you use them to express who you are. However, if you use only those principles adopted or adapted from others, you lose the opportunity to express more of your individual self. Using someone else's principles may limit you in being as aware as possible of your own world. Certainly, your inclusion with the world will lose some of its validity if you rely on the unexamined principles of others. Your whole being must be engaged if you are to clarify the resources needed to truly satisfy your needs. It is your integral self that will sharpen your senses to identify the outcome and resources you need. In other words, there cannot be parts of you that you have ignored or never explored if you are to engage with yourself and the world in a way that is comfortable and fulfilling. You may need to look for new resources. You may need to reach out to others, and you may need to educate yourself on subjects that are new to you. This is how our foundations grow, and our foundations are always growing because our lives are always growing. New activities and new relationships may challenge some of our values and our principles. Honest and authentic awareness can safeguard our integrity and our inner balance.

The foundation of all principles is positive. Any negative statement of principles is not merely the negative of what the principle is, but will always cause confusion about the underlying principle. An example of a negative statement of principle would be "I don't want to hurt wild animals." A positive statement of principle that would encompass the negative principle might be "I am dedicated to the preservation of wild life." The principles that we live with must resonate with our conscious and logical minds, and also fit comfortably with our intuition and unconscious minds. The negative statement of principle is, by its nature, limiting to the conscious mind and, in general, more difficult for the unconscious mind to process. The negative statement of principle is limiting, and it is most likely going to have the opposite of the desired effect. If someone tells you, "don't think about penguins," you are likely to think about penguins. Later on, your unconscious mind may actually remember the statement as an encouragement to think about penguins.

Another aspect of negative principles is that they tend to encourage exclusionary thinking. That is to say they keep you from thinking of things in an embracing way and they encourage you to push things away. Positive statements tend to encourage more positive statements, while negative ones tend to encourage more negative ones. You are much more likely to get what you want by stating positively what you do want rather than by stating what you do not want.

Our lives consist always of the interplay between what we have been taught and what we have learned or are learning on our own. This is true as well of the interplay between what our conscious minds are thinking and what our unconscious minds may be harboring. Finding an internal balance that fits with our integrity is an ongoing and sometimes difficult challenge. The foundation of our principles is a ground that must always shift from time to time. We need to stay aware of our principles as the foundation is changed.

WORKBOOK
Chapter One

1. Can you remember a time when you felt free to explore your world without restrictions? Can you remember when or if that changed? As far as you know, have those changes or lack of changes affected your adult life and in what ways?

2. Have you had the experience of becoming aware that you are aware? Write about times when you have seen your life in a new light. Did those experiences increase your ability to become part of your surroundings?

3. Our principles are derived from our values. Our values do not arise from a vacuum, but are inspired by the observations that come from interactions with the world. Has there ever been a time, perhaps an "a-ha" moment, when you saw things differently? Can you remember how that changed what you valued about those things? What sparked the "a-ha" moment?

4. What is the difference between logic and emotion in in your life? Do you feel a distinct difference? Can you find ways in your life that they are intertwined? Have you ever had a sense of your own "heart consciousness"? How did that fit with your logic and your emotions?

5. Do you have principles that are unique to you as opposed to those derived from others? Are your own principles more important to you than those you received from others? Do they conflict in any way?

6. Practice writing and saying positive and negative statements that apply to your life using the author's examples of a.) "I don't want to hurt wild animals." and b.) "I am dedicated to the preservation of wild life. (Example: I don't want to hurt my kids, or I don't want to fail, or I don't want to be bored.)

2

THE TWO PATHS
OF INCLUSION

*The outward path and the inward path
are two parts of the same path.*

Inclusion blends two paths: one inward and one outward. Both paths are important and both support and develop the human desire for an authentic life. The inward path leads to personal and spiritual growth as well as psychological health and balance. Without a developed and clear inward path leading to balance and health, the outward path will prove to be difficult.

If you have read or studied psychology, psychiatry, religion, or spirituality you probably already have some understanding of what the interior life of a human being looks like. Any thumbnail description will always be woefully inadequate because this is not a simple subject.

In order to understand the inward path of inclusion, there are a few things to consider:

- You are unique.
- Your thoughts and emotions are yours and, therefore, your responsibility.
- You have a heart and feelings that you must learn to access and evolve.
- Emotions play a big part in the structure and quality of your interior life; ignore them at your own peril.

- Your interior life is always woven into and through the world around you as well as the world that you know and experience.

What you know of your interior world and how you come to further understanding depends, in great measure, on how you deal with the influences that you have had in the past and those you will encounter in the future. Although each of us experiences outside influences, that does not alter the fact that how you deal with those influences, in connection to your own development, depends on you, and not the outside influences. They are merely influences; they are not you.

Book after book has been written about the Unconscious, but no one fully understands the intricacies, depth, and scale of the Unconscious. Reading about the interior life can help you know the road, but it is not a substitute for your travels on the road. A full understanding of the interior path can never come from reading and studying alone. It is a path that requires experience to fully understand it.

You have your own dreams. You have an unconscious mind that reveals itself through those dreams, and through your thoughts and emotions that come to you without conscious effort. You cannot expect to know or understand the Unconscious in the same way you understand your conscious mind. The Unconscious exists beyond your conscious mind's grasp.

It is also true that no one can tell you where all aspects of your unconscious mind originate. Suffice it to say, for now, that all you need to know is that the Unconscious does exist, and many of the feelings and thoughts it brings to the fore may seem either unknowable or written in a strange code. The key to a relationship with your Unconscious is to be open to what it has to offer. Especially, when your interior life presents you with quandaries or turmoil, take advantage of its wisdom.

You decide what you like or don't like remembering such that what you prefer one day may well be different o the next. You may have a revelation from one day to the next or you may find that your taste and experience change over time with the choices that you are given. Being open to experience and open to change allows your own attitude and desires to open as well. Principles and, in particular, deep principles must always be tuned to what you know fits well with your hopes, dreams, and desires.

There is the old song from the end of the First World War with these lyrics: "How you gonna keep 'em down on the farm after they've seen Paree?" These lyrics ring true for all of us. Once you have tried new things, it may well be that your mind has been opened and changed about many things in your life.

Personal and psychological problems can be described as a dysfunctional relationship with our internal selves. Personal and psychological problems also carry aspects of the loss of helpful contact with others. In my early years as a parent and young lawyer, I often felt seriously uncomfortable with many parts of myself. I felt lost, in despair, and even worse, that I would never find my way out of my despair. At the time, I did not know that my concern should not have been how to relate to others, but rather how to relate to myself. I developed a serious case of clinical depression with suicidal ideation. Through self-reflection and meditation, I was finally able to start feeling comfortable with myself. Counselors helped by suggesting meditation and teaching me how to listen to my dreams and my unconscious mind, but it was only when I discovered my inward path that I was able to find my way once more. Finding that path helped me find my inner balance.

Powerful principles are cultivated by a balanced self and not a self in turmoil. If by default or by some decision, you have limited yourself to having only certain thoughts or certain experiences, you can well expect both your inner and outer inclusion to be limited. Outer inclusion will always be determined by the extent of your inner inclusion. The quiet stability of inner balance always translates to powerful inclusion with the outer world. To some, it may seem counterintuitive, but you must find your powerful principles through an understanding and enjoyment of yourself.

Our experiences make us who we are. We must learn to savor and enjoy them. I know I would have enjoyed my life much more had I known what I was missing. By worrying so much about the outer world,

I ignored who I was and ended up failing both. Enjoying life and feeling gratitude for our experiences makes us stronger allowing us to discover and cultivate the authentic principles that lead to our ability to create powerful and fulfilling lives.

WORKBOOK
Chapter Two

1. We have identified and listed five key points of the internal path of inclusion. Knowing that you are unique, in what ways do you feel unique? How do you express it? Are you comfortable with it?

2. Your thoughts and emotions are yours and, therefore, your sole responsibility. Do you feel that your thoughts and emotions are your own? Are you comfortable with that? Do you feel that some of your thoughts and emotions are like "hand-me-downs" that never have been incorporated as your own? Can you identify any that you would like to change?

3. You have a heart and feelings that you must learn to access and evolve. Take a few quiet undisturbed minutes, allowing yourself deep and full breaths, and open yourself to the feeling that your heart communicates to you. Can you sense how the cultivation of this connection to your heart could allow you to know more about your desires and your feelings?

4. Emotions play a big part in the structure and quality of your interior life; ignore them at your own peril. Can you think of times that you ignored your emotions? Can you remember the last time you were feeling your own emotions? Are you comfortable feeling your own emotions?

5. Your interior life is always entwined with the surrounding world as well as the world as you know and experience it. Spend a couple of minutes contemplating how your own emotions are connected to others (family, friends, co-workers). Think about how your identity is connected to others. Does anything stand out that helps to define who you are? Are you completely comfortable with this, or are there certain aspects or qualities that feel incomplete or unpleasant?

3

CONTROLLING PERSONAL DESTINY WITH PERSONAL PRINCIPLES

Never underestimate the power of authenticity.
You may not think that you are powerful,
but you will be when you find out who you truly are.

Controlling personal destiny means engaging with the world in a way that aligns with principles that you can truly claim as your own. In part, they may be principles you have learned or adopted from others. These principles become yours when you internalize each, applying and combining them with your own values. Once you do that, these principles become authentic to you and you can claim ownership.

Although we may not be aware of it, there is an emotional basis for all of our principles. As we continue to put our principles into action, emotions continue to play a part in how and where we apply our principles. The emotional basis and overlay of our principles truly have much to do with how effective these principles are when put into action. When emotions are congruent with our thoughts and supportive of our principles in action, there is a much greater likelihood that our actions will be effective and powerful.

When we adopt principles from other individuals, from groups, or from leaders without first applying personal values, we relinquish control and, sooner or later, lose authenticity. The leader of a clique, party, tribe, and even nation can, and often make the effort to wheedle, cajole, seduce, shame, or even brainwash any of us into adopting principles that are not authentic representations of what we want or even need. This kind of situation has surely affected everyone at one time or another. There are some instances in which mind control of others has been horrific. One of the starkest examples of this is the Jonestown Massacre of 1978 where 909 members of a "People's Temple" committed suicide by drinking Kool-Aid mixed with cyanide poison. It is impossible to believe that 909 people would, at the same time, with principles they had examined or embraced, make the decision that mass suicide was the only option. Their minds were made up for them by cult leader, Jim Jones.

Even though most of us will never be under the control of such a diabolical maniac as Jim Jones, the extreme example of Jonestown is important for all of us to understand. Ordinary people are often anxious and even desperate to acquire principles from other people. Indeed, for so many of us, it is daunting or even impossible to critically analyze the principles of influential people or leaders. There are remarkably sad examples of fraternity hazing that end up in serious injury or death. If fraternity members thought about it at all, it would be hard to believe that they would want their actions to lead to the injury of a future member of their own group. These actions must have violated their own principles and, potentially, only satisfied the perverse principles of fraternity leaders in an attempt to control the fraternity. Putting aside the extreme examples of sadism and abuse of others, there is the common tendency on the part of all people to adopt principles from a group, a leader, or a significant person.

"Codependency" is the word for a dysfunctional relationship where one person has given up control of his or her own emotional life to a significant other. Both people can become dependent upon the other for emotional support and sense of self. A dysfunctional couple may not be a case of true codependency, but the boundaries of their emotional selves might be so blurred that they cannot find their way by following their own principles. Until one person in the couple can find the strength of individual principles, the dysfunctional binding cannot be broken. Finding the strength and the courage to implement the principles may lead to the separation of the couple, but the one who finds solid principles will have those to rely upon while proceeding alone.

Frequently, in the cases of political and state power, true-believers give themselves over to the power of the group's leaders whether that be the leader of a party, the president, the king, or, in the case of Adolf Hitler, the fuehrer. We can think of current political affiliations in the same way: followers often are in lock step behind the leader.

In the case of organized religion, true believers are frequently called upon to accept not only the common principles of faith, but also the current leader's interpretation of those principles. History is replete with examples of violent and even grotesque action taken in the name of the major religious faiths of the world. It is unfortunate that this continues into modern times.

The issue is not that it is unusual for people to relinquish the development and control of their own principles, but rather to explain why doing so is common. Perhaps it may be that confronting our own emotions is daunting and even frightening. Often, we lack the capacity to understand our own internal turmoil, and fail to objectively understand our relations with others. Our perception of who we are is often incomplete or waiting for further development, which is why we may be waiting for someone else to fix our futures. Living with someone else's standards may make us so ineffective that we cannot truly finish anything by ourselves.

Although most people have core values, they may not be able to tell you what they are without delving deeply into their lives. Awareness and a depth of introspection is something many people find difficult or disconcerting. It was Oscar Wilde who wrote that a "cynic is a man who knows the price of everything and the value of nothing."

True values and true principles only emerge from an inner understanding, a balanced internal sense of self, and an elementary personal integrity. Understanding, internal balance, and integrity are not just worthy goals, but essential attributes for anyone who wants to develop powerful principles.

WORKBOOK
Chapter Three

1. In your home or work lives have you found yourself in a place where the emotions of others have impacted you? Do you find it difficult to engage from the emotions of others? Write about how you felt, and how you might separate yourself from those emotions if it happens again.

2. Have you been in a personal relationship in which your emotions are so intertwined with the other that you could not find or assert your own identity? How did you disengage from that relationship? Was it easy to find your own resources or was it a struggle for you? Write about how you would like to be able to effectively deal with that kind of problem.

3. Can you think of examples either in your own life or in history when leaders of a group have directed the thinking and the emotions of the group? Are you able to observe how the members of the group have lost some of their individuality?

4. Can you think of times in your past when you have not been able to express your own emotions or your own thinking? Can you see how this affected your ability to authentically express your own principles? How might you address such situations in the future?

4

COMMITMENT

"Shoemaker stick to thy last."
Or the importance of being committed
to what we have chosen to do.

If you are reading this book, you probably have already experienced inclusion in many places in the world. You may have a family, a circle of friends, a job or career, or you might even be a member of a union or church. You may belong to a political party. You may be married or may have been married in the past. You may have a significant other. You probably engage in some kind of social media platforms and you likely send a few or many emails. You understand that these kinds of inclusion have always carried with them some degree of commitment and responsibility to those with whom you have interacted. If your interactions have never required a commitment or any responsibilities, then it is likely that you have acted more from expediency than principle.

You may take inclusion as a given and you may have given little thought to any of its meanings or the importance of inclusivity. Much of our experience of inclusion has been simply by rote and probably according to the expectations of others. Most of it does not engage the full force of our personality and talents nor does it allow for creativity. Many of us already know, consciously or unconsciously, that we don't bring the fullness of who we are into our interaction with the world. Many feel incapable of expressing, or lack a sense of entitlement to our unique character. Lacking a strong sense of who they are, many people can't express what they really want from life, and making commitments can be hard to do.

When someone makes a commitment without knowledge or understanding of his or her own principles, problems arise. Without giving it much thought, a person may have married based solely on who their mother or father wanted them to marry. Many take detrimental actions simply because of "friendly" advice. Children often do this when they accept a dare from one of their peers. Fraternity brothers and sorority sisters gain membership based on taking detrimental and even hazardous actions. Countless people will use alcohol or drugs because someone convinces them to do so. Whether we like it or not, we are the ones who ultimately pay the price and will be responsible for our actions in the end. Sometimes, the consequences last for years and, sometimes, forever.

For nearly everyone, being alone in life is unsatisfying and frustrating. For that reason, everyone seeks inclusion in some fashion. However, inclusion is difficult when natural relationships that would comfortably foster inclusion are minimized or eliminated. In general, the feeling of belonging to a tribe or to a larger group has been severely diminished in the recent past. We live in a fast-paced world of huge cities, we drive around alone in our cars, we live alone, or are lonely in our lives. Millions of people now find their social connections through messages using only 140 characters. The internet has allowed us to have social interaction, but it can also be shallow and ephemeral.

Many others are caught on the horns of the dilemma of responsibilities for their jobs and careers, or for their children from a failed or failing relationship and don't have the social network that would support their ability to comfortably fulfill their responsibilities. This can make a person feel lost. What happens to principled inclusion when that happens?

A true and congruent self is the core inspiration and original resource for principled inclusion. When something is forced on you, it is hard or even impossible to find internal congruence. It may well seem impossible to act upon powerful principles when you feel either very lonely or that circumstances are forcing you to do things that you either don't want to do or can only do with great difficulty. When these kinds of situations arise, it is best to find support within yourself by understanding the essence of who you are. The result of seeking integrity and internal congruence creates the emergence of the powerful principles that will see you through. Surprisingly, in the most trying times, you may have the best opportunity to develop your true and powerful principles.

You may have, as I have had, highly committed relationships that fail. You may even work at more than one career in your lifetime. No matter the upheavals and changes in fortune and fate, the constant in your life must be your principles. Even through the most trying times, I can look back seeing that I was able to make it through and even thrive by sticking with what I knew was congruent or fitting with my principles. Keep true to what is motivating and fulfilling. Use that motivation and fulfillment to direct the purposes and activities that need your commitment. Be prepared to give all you reasonably can, but don't ever forget the principles that will make you effective and powerful in what you have committed to do. Remember, our final commitment must be to our principles.

WORKBOOK
Chapter Four

1. Think back on some of the important relationships of your life with family and loved ones. Can you feel that inclusion now? Write down the "rules" that you were following and how they let you express your identity or how they limited it.

2. When you formed new relationships, did you feel the commitment you made was truly your own idea or were you expressing the will and the principles of others? How do you think this limited yourself and the relationship?

3. Can you see how the limitations of past relationships also limited your inclusion in other relationships? What are your thoughts about that?

4. Have you had times when you felt lost and alone? Can you think about what role you played in your own loneliness? Were there ways you could have changed your internal view of yourself and been happier even though you were alone?

5. Can you see how the ways you were thinking at the time were the application of principles to yourself? Does this give you a sense of how principles can be developed, changed, and applied?

5

INCLUSION
WITH THE WORLD

*Seek the power of your
authentic self's expression.*

How many of us have done the same thing over and over out of sheer habit? How many of us ignore any creative input accepting the same thing we have always received? How many of us don't even know that something different is possible?

Much of our inclusion with the world has been received without any input from us. We do what we do without much new thought or authentic emotion. We function on autopilot with little direction or awareness that a new way of being is possible. Changing our hairstyle or buying a new set of clothes won't do much to alter a life that lacks meaning, and is unlikely to make a more effective human being. You can't expect to make meaningful, not to mention long-term, changes in life without critical analysis and perspective. Objective awareness of ourselves and the way we are living can take our heads out of the clouds and away from disturbing and even entrancing narcissistic thinking. Objective awareness opens the way for personal discernment which leads to an authentic relationship to an inner life. This creates a connection to meaning, purpose, and authentic expression.

From this awareness, we derive powerful principles that enable effective interaction with our world. The question is not whether we need an authentic connection to ourselves, but rather how to know when we are not being authentic, and then how to set about creating change when we might have some doubts about our own authenticity. It's a conundrum. To be true to ourselves is to be aware that what we are doing or saying might not feel comfortable or ring true to personal authenticity. A life built on the shifting sands of falsehood cannot nourish the foundation of powerful principles.

If you encounter a person or situation that makes you feel uneasy, ask yourself why. If you encounter someone or something that feels stale, exhausted, inadequate, distorted, or out of proportion to what feels right, ask yourself why. If that question is not quickly answered, calmly give yourself some distance and perspective. Ask yourself: What am I sensing? How does it sit with my heart? With my intuition? There is no good substitute for self-examination. It provides you with a chance to reassert what you want or discover what you need. Honest self-examination points you towards new principles or helps change and adapt previously held principles. In the process of self-examination, be aware that your principles must guide you.

Crucial factors in our development or potential such as where we are born and to whom, what kind of schools we attend, our gender and how we look physically, are typically not left up to us to decide. This part of our histories did not include much, if any, creative input on our part. It just happened, and some might feel that it just happened *to* us. The good news is that this way of thinking and living can change by developing creativity and activating your creative potential as a part of life.

Creative input is possible when we become aware of our interior life and work toward finding and keeping true to personal integrity. Making your mark and being powerful in the world will not be an accident. The ways in which we present ourselves will, in large measure, determine the welcome we get and the invitations we receive to be included in the world. Actions that are supported by principle always have a better chance of being recognized. When they are carried out with a desire to be included, and an indication of the benefits one wishes to have, there is a much greater likelihood of achieving success.

Many books have been written about the law of attraction, which means attracting what you want by thinking about and wishing for it. Principled inclusion expands upon that concept by underscoring the importance of being fully who you want to be and who you are fully meant to be. It assumes that what you want from the world will follow from who you are and, as you more fully engage with the world, that you will continue to invite what you want. It assumes that we continue to evolve all aspects of ourselves and that how we engage the world will, thereby, change over time. Focusing only on what we want to attract is a poor substitute for focusing on who we truly are. Concentrating on the reward may well interfere with the performance. Any applause that comes our way must not be a substitute for the music we perform. Instead of looking outside for appreciation, remember that the appreciation we have for ourselves is key to success and happiness. By balancing external adulation with ample self-examination, we find the parts of ourselves that lead to happiness.

In other words: Don't chase happiness. Let it catch up to you. As you develop and apply principled inclusion, it will determine who or what you are meant to serve. You can then give it all the attention you have. The proper rewards will follow because these principles are the expression of your entire self. Allow for these important changes without focusing on potential feedback alone.

An authentic inner life plays a key role in determining our principles. We receive direction if we listen to the voice that connects to personal authenticity. That voice may come from intuition, our unconscious mind, or from an external source. Sometimes it comes from sage advice and counseling. Sometimes it comes from reading or something we see in the media. Sometimes it comes from prayer, or from what could be called a divine or transcendent source. It is our responsibility to pay attention and to listen and become aware of the signs and signals as to the direction we should follow.

Although thought and emotion are important factors in defining who we are, neither adequately accounts for the complexity of any human being. We are so much more than what we think or feel. In our search for an authentic self, it is essential that we be open to aspects of who we are, even those that may be muddled and unclear. By being open to understanding ourselves, we create an opportunity for previously unknown aspects of ourselves to be revealed. Principles that fit our needs are the most effective.

Abraham Lincoln famously said, "You can fool all of the people some of the time, and some of the people all the time, but you cannot fool all the people all the time." He was of the opinion that eventually people do discover when someone is trying to fool or mislead them.

Throughout history and even in contemporary times, startling examples exist of people finding out, way too late, that they are being misled or fooled. Jim Bakker, an infamous televangelist with a huge following, is one fairly recent example who was discovered to be a fraud and, later, convicted on charges of fraud. Bakker not only preached principles he evidently did not believe, he also was content to mislead others in his sociopathic plans. In the short term, Bakker acquired great wealth, but it did not last once he was discovered and exposed.

On the other hand, we have sterling examples of those who maintained and evolved their principles to achieve advancement and the advancement of the multitudes that they influenced. One such example is Winston Churchill who evolved his principles over many decades to more and more effectively serve Great Britain. Mohandas Gandhi is another. From a legal career in South Africa, Gandhi became the foremost leader of modern India. Legend has it that Siddhartha Gautama Buddha, the founder of Buddhism, did the same as he evolved from being a prince in India to become the sage who explained our mystical connection to the world. Every era has had incredible examples of people with improbable beginnings who became profound leaders in their time. Every family has a story of some family member, past or present, who underwent great changes. Psychologists, psychiatrists, analysts, mentors, counselors of all types, and many others assist in the creative change process.

It may be difficult to develop new ways of thinking or creative, emotional paths when we are tripping over the old ones. Self-examination and self-acceptance help us to push beyond overpowering thoughts and emotions. It is important to pay attention to interfering thoughts and emotions, but not allow them to control you. Remember that interfering thoughts are still our own and, therefore, we have a responsibility for them. By following the interference and attempting to understand it, we can gain control of it. As we dispel fear, we may locate the source and possible direction of it. Being aware of it makes us less vulnerable. If you don't feel that you can face your fears alone, ask for help. Asking for help opens you to accepting help and to accepting your own fears.

Finding and keeping powerful inclusive principles requires openness, awareness, and the willingness to admit that you need to grow and change. While still maintaining a strong sense of personal understanding and integrity, principled inclusion requires extending yourself to as many other humans and as much of life as possible. The mere willingness to do so will expand both your internal boundaries and those boundaries surrounding you.

WORKBOOK
Chapter Five

1. Write about a time when being in touch with your authentic self would have been beneficial.

2. Is it possible that there are times when being authentic might make life harder?

3. Have you had such experiences in terms of standing up for your ideals?

4. Are there people in your life who inspire you? Who are they? Do they contribute to your own sense of authenticity?

5. Can you think of people in your life, or leaders you have known, who were not authentic?

6. Have you experienced a time when you set your mind to something and got it? Can you sense how you "attracted" this to yourself?

7. Can you sense the difference between getting something because you wanted it, and getting something because you effectively acted on your own principles?

6

POWERFUL INCLUSION

There are dynamic and effective ways
to be truly powerful in the world.

Powerful inclusion in the world can be learned, cultivated, and refined. Over the millennia that human culture has existed, powerful inclusion has been discovered by people everywhere. Those who have achieved inclusion may not be able to articulate how they achieved it, but the steps they have taken to get there are almost always similar. Many who achieve partial inclusion may stumble or fall before realizing what has happened or before having the time to appreciate the changes that even partial inclusion brings to any one life. For some, inclusion will fail for lack of adapting to the world. Powerful inclusion in the world is not a final state of being, but rather a description of a dynamic and effective interaction with the outer world.

To be powerfully included, you must understand and enjoy the world. You cannot be effective in your principled action without extensive understanding of what your world is made of. History provides many unique and impressive examples of powerful and principled people whose lives displayed an understanding of the world that allowed them to form strong and effective principles and, later, put them into action. Three great, well-known examples include George Washington, Franklin Roosevelt, and Booker T. Washington. All three men spent decades learning about their world while cherishing and enjoying it. A reading of a short biography of each shows how extensive was their desire to experience and learn about the world around them. Undoubtedly, they would not have been able to serve as the brilliant examples of principled people without their literal hands-on grasp of the world they each inhabited. Each man showed how their appreciation of their world and eventual deep gratitude opened the way for them to powerfully influence their spheres of experience and influence. None would have been able to jump from the early exploration of their worlds to their eventual leadership roles without these experiences. The importance of vast life experience cannot be overstated.

To the end of their lives, all three dynamic leaders continued to develop and perfect their principles. The same holds true for all human beings: Principles develop throughout a lifetime, and change as we grow or are the very elements that allow us to grow.

As our personal integration changes and as we adapt, our interactions with the world change as well. For every example of a leader who has successfully adapted their principles to achieve ever greater accomplishments, there are examples of those who have refused to do so. This non-adaptive approach is usually detrimental. Perhaps the issue for these leaders was in being stubbornly fixated or enamored of their principles, and not allowing new insights to challenge or amend their principles.

To be sure, there are those with perfectly good and strong principles who were not able to achieve inclusion. Many principled human beings have died in prison or in conflict, alone or with a few other people, because their principles and actions were not accepted in their time and place. When actions are based on principled integrity, their appropriateness is unquestionable. Powerful principles are not themselves the assurance of "success". It is suggested that true and abiding success happens only with powerful principles.

For all of us, some of our principles may seem contradictory from time to time. For all of us, it is important to develop a sense of the difference between what our hearts tell us and what our minds and our "common sense" tell us. Not following our hearts is known to have serious consequences. Not thinking about what we are doing also is known to have serious consequences. Furthermore, social convention may carry some adverse consequence if we don't follow what is the consensus of "common sense". Balancing the interests and the influences of our lives is an art. When there is a doubt on how to proceed, wait for calmness and inspiration. Be compassionate with yourself and as compassionate as you can be with others. Listen to your heart along with your intuition. This will greatly clarify your best direction.

We cannot be in a position to fully and effectively engage the world unless we have an ongoing intensive interaction with the world. We cannot appreciate something we don't know in depth. Neither can we fully appreciate nor be grateful for anything we have not encountered close up. Deeply experiencing our world is something all of us must do throughout our lives if we are to have principled inclusion in the world. The deeper our experience of the world, the greater our understanding. Certainly, the same is true of ourselves. Since gratitude is the ultimate result of deep experience of the world, we can look on the entirety of our experience as "the realm of gratitude." Organizing a world view around this way of thinking will tend to make you more receptive to deep appreciation of what you are given in life.

The world view of gratitude is based, first of all, on an understanding and appreciation of what we possess. This recognition can be as wide as the recognition that we live on a gorgeous, blue orb that supports the teaming life forms of over 8 million species of animals and plants. It can also be as specific as appreciating the clothes you have on your back. We cannot know or count our "blessing" unless we know what we possess. This may be only stating the obvious, but it is the obvious that is often disregarded when we take our world for granted. Often times, we don't really appreciate what we have until it is taken from us. Deep appreciation of your world is the first step toward understanding who you are. It is the first step to solving the turmoil and turbulence you may face. It is also the first step toward your spiritual growth, if that is your inclination.

From appreciation, we learn that we can work on our internal balance by exercising compassion. Compassion is the understanding of the emotions of ourselves and others. We can approach this compassion because we are aware and grateful for the world around us. By embracing our world and being open to the thoughts and emotions of others, we give ourselves a break from the conflict and turbulence in our lives allowing it to rest. Compassion helps to free us from the attachments we have to others that do not allow us to be comfortable with our authentic selves. This personal compassion creates the opportunity to feel what we need to then create balance and integrity in our lives.

By truly seeing the world as something worthy of gratitude, your senses and awareness remain as open as possible. When you are as aware as you can be, in both your sense of yourself and of the world around you, the principles that resonate with your values and your integrated self will be more easily found and more easily implemented. This can and should be done with a full engagement and savoring of the wonders of the world. To miss the opportunity to fully savor your world is to lose the huge opportunities of enjoyment offered.

Principles are not easily defined, and differ from person to person. Principles can be rules to live by, emotions that motivate you, emotions that define how you interpret and interact with the world, sensibilities, or morals. Principles are often the same as ethics. They are even represented in what you eat and the way you eat it. They are very much the attitudes that you have adopted in your life. As we go about our daily lives, we pick and choose or automatically engage with myriad principles. Principles define our politics whether or not we acknowledge that to be true, and reveal our method of dealing with the world. Sometimes, under stress, our principles can change drastically, or they can be very resistant to change.

To the extent that we wish to be self-actuated and self-aware, we must attempt to sense, comprehend and evaluate our principles. The brilliance of our minds can be used to put some logical framework around why we do what we do. This is highly recommended for achieving mindfulness and self-awareness. However, the mind without the involvement of the heart will likely give a false reading as to what your true motivating principles are. Even the mind in tandem with the heart will often give false readings unless the mind is encouraged to slow its involvement or remove its immediate critical judgment. Even the use of the word "encourage"

– which means to engage the heart – shows how we intuitively know that our heart and our emotions direct who we are.

Intuition plays a big part in our values and principles. We need our hearts and the neurology of our entire body to be intuitive. Believers in transcendent spirits and in the Great Creator will usually tell you that the heart is where the messages, strengths, and directions originate for the purposes we need to assume in our principled life. We often say that if it does not fit with your "gut," then don't do it. Likewise, if it does not "feel" right, then don't do it either.

If the truth were known, our emotions hold the secrets to the strength of our values. Our values and sensibilities form the basis of support for our moral codes. Our moral codes often are dictated by social and group norms that require our subscription and enforcement for their vitality. When values and sensibilities turn against norms or moral codes, there is likely a quick change coming. This is true both for individuals and for groups.

Principles are the written or unwritten, the articulated or non-articulated methods and prescriptions that individuals use in social interaction. Principles can be the methods that individuals or couples use, that small groups use, or that an entire society uses for prescribed and unspoken interaction. Written laws are social codifications of principles. Methods of social courtesy and social grace are other examples of unwritten principles. We have hundreds, if not thousands, of principles that we use as part of our operational manual for social interaction. Yet, for the vast percentage of us, there are relatively few principles that form the basis, or the trunk of the tree, of our methods of social interaction.

Core principles are the ones that energize and support all other principles of daily existence. Core principles form the basis for taking the actions that we take. You can identify your core principles in the ways that they force you to pay attention. Love and respect for my family and dignity for myself and those around me are among my core principles. Core principles also direct us in identifying and seeking personal goals. One of my goals is to protect those who are most vulnerable and most in need. That goal is based on my core principles of dignity, honor, and health for all. When we base our goals on core principles, we can comfortably find the internal and external resources for the achievement of our goals. Being aware of core principles is an important part of finding the principles of powerful inclusion with the world. The goal is always to find and maintain internal balance and personal integrity. Checking in with your core principles from time to time will keep you focused on what is important to you. Communicating those principles through words and actions adds to your effectiveness.

Throughout life, we belong to or participate in many groups such as family and friends, places of worship, clubs, schools, neighborhoods, political parties, and co-workers. With each group, we may find differences in terms of the principles we share. How strongly we hold to those principles, and how precisely and consistently we apply these principles determines how powerfully they affect any particular group. For principles to be powerful, they must be emotionally and personally congruent, apply to group action in a consistent and sensible way, and inspire the group to attain a level of integrity. An old expression says, "There is honor even among thieves." Honor is one way of saying that there are recognizable principles that even thieves are expected to maintain.

For principles to be powerful, they do not, necessarily, have to be intentionally forged in the crucible of your heart. They can be acquired over time. You might even think your way into principles that are highly effective and powerful. What matters is that they be principles you can use to engage the world that allow you to be internally congruent with your actions. They cannot be truly powerful if they are contradictory with the many parts of yourself. They are powerful when they show fortitude and dedication.

We cannot be enthusiastic about principles that do not make sense at a conscious level, nor can we be enthusiastic about principles that do not sit well emotionally and spiritually. If things that you are doing, or that are happening around you, make you feel bad or make you feel insecure, it is a good time to take an internal assessment of your principles. Everyone must do that from time to time.

Searching for the appropriate principles will inevitably bring us back to our core. It will take us back to the basic values and sensibilities that form the basic support for emotional and cognitive interaction. Answers tend to emerge from an internal conversation with your true self rather than an external search.

Truly influential and powerful people have achieved the kind of internal integrity and congruence that allows the social presentation of the one who knows and the one who truly believes. This is the mark of the leader and successful doer, and the one who knows how to control or strongly influence the group. The strongest member of a group can frequently be the most dedicated and purposeful member of the group, and not necessarily the designated leader. How many times have you known a janitor of a school who over the years has come to show such dedication and caring the he or she is looked to for both moral and actual support? Probably many times.

Our life principles fit together like a narrative or story. The more varied and complicated the life, the more likely there will be many principles and some variation among them. It is the responsibility of each of us who desires principles to examine them from time to time to assure enough consistency and to avoid hypocrisy.

For many of us, a greater ideal is beckoning. If we are to be effective and powerful, we must be aware of all influences that call us to greater ideals. For those people who are aware of that calling, be aware as well that there is no time to delay. Those who are most powerful will listen and then take action.

WORKBOOK
Chapter Six

1. What are your core values or principles?

2. Make a list of each core value.

3. How have they changed during your life?

4. How have they stayed the same?

5. Are you able to apply your core principles in every situation in which you find yourself?

6. Can you remember a time when your actions contradicted your values? Can you remember how that felt?

7. What greater ideal calls you? Is there more than one? Can you imagine how you would act on those ideals?

7

SELF-AWARENESS

Spending time understanding your surroundings
as well as understanding and acquiring your
wants and needs is never time wasted.

Personal power depends on self-acceptance. You cannot grow into your fullest potential unless you accept all parts of yourself. As you become more aware of yourself and your surroundings, you can also be more aware of your strongest principles. Your increased awareness will allow you to know how and when to apply those principles most effectively.

Awareness of yourself and your surroundings will help you find the resources that you need to enjoy your world and express yourself. If you find yourself lacking in resources, take the time to find out what it is that limits you and your internal self. If you believe that resources are so scarce that you cannot provide for yourself and others, your limited thinking has misled you. In the book of Matthew in the New Testament of the Christian Bible, you'll find the quote: "Seek and ye shall find." Many spiritual thinkers have insisted that abundant thinking brings resources whereas limited thinking, or what is also known as poverty conscious-ness, brings exactly that: poverty and scarcity. You live with an internal genius and that part of you can and will discover resources and methods available to provide for both yourself and others. Whatever the origins of your resources, expect that your request and search will bring results. The mere act of asking for the fulfillment of your needs will be the start of your finding them. This is no accident and does not involve magic. It is the act of self-realization.

Finding your true potential is one of your tasks in life. Assistance from others is vital, but will never be an appropriate substitute for finding your internal core. This requires that you be as aware as possible of your own needs. Being aware of yourself and your surroundings means subjecting yourself to a scrutiny that rejects quick answers. There are many reasons why it may be difficult to be aware of why we do what we do. Sometimes, we simply don't know what we want, and when and if we do, we might not know how to get it, and may even find ourselves doing things repeatedly with less than optimal results. The roots of our patterns of struggle can be so deep and widespread that we are dumbfounded as to how to seek a change. In order to achieve meaningful change or meaningful resolution, it might be necessary to seek assistance from a third party such as a counselor or spiritual leader. Whether you do that or not, you will need to sharpen your awareness by calmly opening your senses.

Calmness is a skill used most effectively when seeking change, and requires that we hone our skills to achieve such a state. As with most skills, calmness gets better, stronger, and more immediately available when we develop it. It is a deep subject worthy of much more analysis, but it is sufficient enough to know that the ability to become calm, and using calmness to form the basis of your principles and your decisive actions, cannot be overstated. The more you develop the skills to achieve calmness, the better you will be at using calmness for resolving personal issues.

From a state of calmness, you will be in a much better place to ask questions, even if your question is only "How can I resolve the feeling I have?" We really need calmness when we seek answers to questions about our feelings. It is important, too, to ask ourselves questions without preconceived notions of what answers may come. Setting aside preconceived notions potentially opens us to receiving answers from multiple sources that may come to us from outside ourselves or it may come from an internal source, such as our intuition. We may find changes in our personality that we were not expecting and could not predict. Those who are spiritually inclined may find changes coming from a transcendental source.

The openness that can come from awareness and receptivity leads towards more people, more groups, more life in general, and more intense and satisfying relationships with people and life. The goal is always a fuller, richer, more flavorful life in whatever way you personally define it.

Richness and flavor may well evade you if you do not take the time to savor and learn to enjoy your world. Savoring takes time. Discover the flavor and beauty of life and the world around you through the process of savoring. From this savoring, you will discover or reaffirm the principles that you will use to influence the world. Your attention helps you see the dimensions and complexity of the world you encounter. The deeper, greater, and fuller your awareness, knowledge, and experience with your world, the easier it will be to find the principles that support the creation of effectiveness and power in your world.

WORKBOOK
Chapter Seven

1. Have you had the opportunity to identify your personal resources? What are they? How are they useful?

2. Think of a recent situation and ask yourself how you could have looked for resources that would have made you more effective? Even if it involves some wishful thinking, be creative. Does this give you clues for the future?

3. How do you understand calmness? What does it mean to you? How can you achieve calmness more readily?

4. Do you have thoughts that limit your life? What are they?

5. Do you know your true potential? How have you limited it in the past?

6. Make a list of ways you could better savor your life, and think about adding to this every day for a month, two months, or even a year. Keep your list handy!

8

PREPARING FOR
EMPOWERMENT

If you want to win,
stop trying and start doing!

For those of you who believe it is pretentious to think of yourself as powerful, please put that thought to the side. Certainly, it would be misguided, even silly, to start life thinking of yourself as uniquely powerful and, therefore, not accountable to others for your behavior. Yet, as you grow and mature, you have the need and the right to be effective in life. You not only have the need, but the obligation, to fulfill responsibilities that you have either accepted or that are expected of you in your life situations. Additionally, you have the right to whatever influence reasonably comes your way. It is difficult to achieve much in life without a measure of confidence in the ability to do so. Even a person with extensive education and training may find it difficult to be effective and powerful without confidence. Confidence evolves from some degree of internal balance along with the courage to believe in yourself. We think of confidence as having faith and belief in oneself, but the deeper meaning is to believe in or *with* yourself.

As you know yourself better, and know the importance of your own feelings, you will feel more capable of seeking and asking for what you want from yourself and others. Discovering your most effective voice means, first, learning what you truly have to say. What is unique about you? What is important? Doing the most effective things you can means discovering and understanding the things you really want to do. Being the most effective human being in all situations means being who you truly want to be and truly are. Finding, developing, and keeping true to our most authentic self is, without a doubt, the most difficult, and yet the most important, task of our lives. Rejections and failures can make us think we are ineffective in certain situations and certain activities. For instance, not being loved at key times in our lives can lead us to think we cannot and will not ever be loved, or truly loved, for who we are.

Even though being effective in the world is a worthy goal, our first responsibility is to ourselves. This is true—if for no other reason—that to be as effective as possible, we must first be as capable, collected, developed, and balanced as possible. Other people and situations we encounter in life are often instrumental to our personal development though, at its core, inner development involves our own personal work. You have to be prepared and capable of finding and knowing yourself if you are to join the world in a powerfully inclusive way.

Many of us find it daunting to think about what we want and who we truly are. People can even be afraid to find out who they truly are. For many, it is better to believe what others have taught them to be, better to act out their lives with the script provided, and better to avoid identifying who they might really want to be, rather than becoming their true and real self. Maybe the real, authentic self seems uncontrollable and, maybe, a bit too messy. Don't worry, you'll learn that the mess is ready and waiting for you to arrange it in ways that nourish and satisfy your personal needs and tastes.

No one should tell us what we like to eat, how to dress, what kinds of friends to have, or how to arrange our lives. Certain things are just too personal for outside interference. You are truly important, and deep down you must allow yourself to comfortably and confidently accept that. Personal importance may start with dreaming, but it must also be accompanied by integrity and abiding principles combined with congruent and directed action. If you want something, there's a good chance that you will have to act to get it. To have something worth having requires giving something of yourself. What you give must come from you and you alone without intimidation from others. What you give must fit comfortably with your principles.

Each of us finds personal values and principles in unique ways seeing who we are in different lights and from differing perspectives. Some people align themselves with a religious or spiritual method. Others seek contact with their intuition, or a method of connecting to an internal voice. We are each free to make choices and so, whichever method or technique works for the individual should be the method used. You may arrive at something uniquely your own, or you may find great substance in lessons others give you. It matters not where those sources come from, but rather whether the values and principles give meaning and substance to your life. The power that you find in your life will depend less on where you find your integrity than what you do with it once it is found.

Preparing yourself for empowerment means being ready to confront, absorb, and even analyze your emotions and the emotions of others. To be effective and powerful will require that you exercise your emotional intelligence seeking internal growth that points you towards your true feelings. This emotional intelligence requires you to be ready to feel what you are feeling while also recognizing and trying to understand the feelings of those you encounter. That feeling is called "compassion" or "to feel with," and it is not the feeling that comes from pity or sympathy, but, instead, an acknowledgment that your feelings and the feelings of others are important and must be respected.

You cannot be effective in your interior life or in your relations with others without a grasp of your emotional state and the emotional position of others. Ignoring or disrespecting the feelings of others or yourself can have multiple negative consequences including that you will miss the true meaning of a specific situation and even your life. You cannot be powerful in your principles if there is not a healthy relationship or inclusion of emotions. That said, none of us should be bound up or bogged down by our own or anyone else's emotions. We all need to engage emotions in whatever way the situation requires, but nothing more than that. Just as our emotions must be balanced within our integral self, emotions should be balanced in social situations as well.

Being aware of other peoples' emotions offers release from the types of emotional attachment that do not serve personal growth and integrity. Being as aware as you can be of your emotions allows you to be free from detrimental emotional energy. It also allows you to find out what your real needs and goals are. All of this takes perspective. Emotions can free you or they can get you stuck, and you will not become unstuck or break free without first gaining perspective.

Freeing yourself means giving credence to and respect for your emotions. Freeing yourself means recognizing the feelings of others along with the realization that those emotions belong to them and not you. Your ability to grasp the emotional aspect of any situation cannot be underestimated. If calmness, self-reflection, and an internal inventory do not extricate you from enmeshed emotions, ask for help and seek resources wherever you can find them.

Once freed from emotional turmoil, you will, more and more, find yourself in the presence of your true self. As your life unfolds, your process of inclusion continues to unfold as well, and you will find your life filling with more of what you need. Integrity and abiding principles will attract what you need because you are ready and have dispelled disbelief. Gratitude, calmness, and compassion for self and others, and a belief in oneself brings greater and greater inclusion. Inclusion breeds inclusion. Connection breeds connection. Be ready.

WORKBOOK
Chapter Eight

1. Reflect upon the major groups that have influenced your life. What have they required of you? Have you always been happy about those requirements?

2. Do you feel that you have unique qualities that have not been appreciated or accepted?

3. Has this ever happened to you: "Not being loved at key times in our lives, for instance, can lead us to think we cannot or will not ever be loved, or truly loved, for who we are."? Do those experiences still influence how you move through the world? How you feel about yourself now?

4. Have you ever felt that a special person, family member or some other important person did not love you or appreciate you for who you truly are? If so, does that feeling affect the way you interact with others now?

5. Do you have any fears about discovering your true self? Do you think that you have any fears about encountering some emotions or aspects of yourself? Is there something about yourself that you would not want to share with others? Do you feel that you are integrating the parts of yourself that you don't like to share with others? Does this limit your encounters with others?

6. Does this ring true for you: "Maybe the real, authentic self seems uncontrollable and, maybe, a bit too messy." How might you imagine arranging that mess to nourish your personal growth?

7. Are there are aspects of yourself that you have not been able to fully accept, and that you don't share with others? Has this affected your ability to be authentic with others?

9

SHAPING
YOUR WORLD

*You are powerful enough to shape
the world into something you truly want.*

How you relate to and integrate with others will shape, and possibly dictate, what you get in return. How you relate to and integrate with the world will also shape both what you want and what you will receive. How you accept and integrate all parts of yourself will shape how you live life and determine your integrity. You cannot expect to know yourself without exploring all aspects of yourself. And because we don't live in a vacuum, our personalities, characters, and, indeed, all that we consider to be our total selves are shaped by what and how we learn from others.

We live in a world of vast resources and a feast for the senses with nearly infinite experiences that provide the basis for enjoyment and growth in all aspects of life. Every experience gives us the opportunity to add to what we already have and to grow into what we might become. From these experiences, we learn what is good and bad along with the many shades of difference between the two. We learn what causes sadness, joy, fear, and excitement. We learn how to express the natural urges and natural emotions of our innate nature. Without the experiences we have had with the world, we could not feel awe, gratitude, or love. Even for those who find a transcendent spirit or force that provides answers that reach far beyond themselves, they still must return to the world they live in, which is the world of experience. Powerful principles are always connected to aspects of our experiences that we want to encourage, shape, modify, or eliminate. Even a transcendent influence must connect to our physical world in some meaningful way. Every belief source and every method of inspiration mediates through experience. Gratitude and Love are related experiences. In these transcendent realms, we experience the feelings of Awe, Gratitude, and Love. Experience is the teacher and we always return to experience to understand what motivates us, what is important to us, and what our values and principles mean.

Interactions with the physical world can either carry us along — acting only upon us — or they can be something that we fashion ourselves. The world will always shape us if we, ourselves, do not have a plan of action or ways to develop abilities to shape the world. If we make it clear to the world what we expect and how we expect it, we have a good chance of getting something near to what we ask for.

The ultimate truth is that it is personal life principles that will most strongly shape what you get from life and how you experience it. Although you might think that expedient, immediate satisfaction will be the most beneficial, any results will be temporary and likely to send you on a trajectory of unknown consequences. Something may seem like a deal, or the deal may become its own justification, but you should always consider the possible immediate and long-term consequences. There is an old saying: "The best deal is the one you passed up." None of us can know all the consequences of our actions because we do not know the future. However, when you take actions that fit your life principles, the outcomes are much more predictable and much more likely to have long-term personal satisfaction as an end result.

My grandmother used to say: "Beware of what you ask for, because you just might get it." She would say that our requests are often answered, even if we have not carefully considered the consequences. We have all heard stories of lottery winners who find that being rich does not fit with who they are, or who they want to be. These "lucky folks" often end up giving the money away or losing all of it. What we truly want is something that connects with and helps evolve our core values. Lottery winners have applied quickly acquired principles to the old values and found them wanting. The same thing can happen when we find a new paramour who does not fit with what our heart truly wants. If there is no heart connection, the relationship will falter or fail entirely.

We don't buy our principles in a store. We can't force them to satisfy our whims or expedient needs. Our principles must be an expression of our true selves. We must share in their authorship. Others will certainly contribute to both our principles and understanding of them, but before they become effectively our own, we must adapt them to who we are. Adversity often helps us to refine or readjust our principles. For example, if we are unjustly accused of a crime, we might adjust our principles as related to authority. We might have a new feeling dealing with the needy or the homeless if ever we are in the same predicament. It is up to each of us to figure out what principles we will adopt.

The old song goes: "Into each life some rain must fall." Surely, we shouldn't wish troubles on others, but it pays to be aware that troubles often challenge people to where their values, principles, intuition, and deep emotions intersect at the core. It challenges the core because the core is where our principles are always tested. Challenging events in our lives give us a great opportunity to identify what is most important to us, and a reminder of what we may be missing, or may have forgotten. Negative aspects of challenging events can point you in the direction of what is positive within your core. Response to adversity can either affirm your principles, or help you forge new ones that fit with your developed core.

WORKBOOK
Chapter Nine

1. Can you identify experiences that helped shape who you are? Can you sense how they affected or developed "parts" of you? Do you keep yourself open to new experiences that may yet affect who you are and that can add to the parts of yourself?

2. Have you had adversity in your life? How did it affect you? Did you use it to include yourself further in the world or did you let it limit you? If adversity has limited you, can you think of ways it might be re-examined to help bring you closer to others?

3. Do you have a personal definition of your spiritual nature? Is it different or the same as when you were a child? A younger adult? Is there a spiritual side of yourself? Are you using the spiritual side of yourself to develop yourself? Does the spiritual side help you include or exclude others in your life?

4. What would you do if you won the lottery? Make a list. What could you do on that list without winning the lottery? Does everything on that list fit with your core values and principles?

10

GRATITUDE

Experience begets understanding,
which begets appreciation, which begets gratitude.
Taken together, these define the realm of gratitude.

The secret to finding ourselves or to accessing our interior world always begins with appreciation and direct experience of the outer world. This includes the words we learn and speak, the food we eat, the places we live, as well as the outer world we see, hear, smell, touch, and experience. Learning about, experiencing, and savoring the world around us inspires gratitude, and gratitude, in turn, allows us to embrace and enjoy the world around us. Through a lifetime of experiencing the wonders and joys of life and the Earth, we find ourselves in the "realm" of gratitude. This realm opens the way for the discovery and appreciation of aspects of ourselves that connect and find satisfaction with all aspects of the world. Through our experiences, we literally incorporate ourselves into the world, and by allowing ourselves to be receptive to gratitude, we open more fully into our interior and exterior worlds. Perhaps, more fundamentally, gratitude is the foundation for both our physical and spiritual existences. It is the air we breathe, the food we eat, and the defining experience that shapes who we are and how we are able to be grateful. If you don't have anything to be grateful for, then perhaps you need to change your experiences, or perhaps open your senses to more fully appreciate what you are experiencing.

Understand that all of this is your responsibility. How many are there in the world who, like me, have spent so much time attempting to experience and achieve more and more, without taking the time to understand or appreciate those experiences or accomplishments? How many like me who have let so many things in life pass by without taking the time or even knowing how to understand or appreciate life? One way to change is through the act of observing the world. Observation and awareness are key. Life is in the journey, not the destination. By taking the time to smell a rose, we can sense what the rose actually is. By studying a beautiful painting, we can appreciate the gifts of the artist and the painting itself. Those kinds of actions open us to the realm of gratitude.

By listening, tasting, smelling, and experiencing the outer world, you enter the realm of gratitude because listening, tasting, smelling, and experiencing are the requirements. If you desire food, savor each bite, but don't give way to gluttony. If you desire intimacy, be amorous without becoming overwhelmed. Always remember to savor experience no matter what because savoring helps you discover the more exquisite aspects of experience.

By learning to experience the outer world, you develop principles of personal involvement. Be as aware as possible of what is being experienced. Be aware of what principles are being taught and what principles are being accepted. Savor the experience and learn what you like and don't like. Remember that excess often leads to either exhaustion or internal discord derived from excess: excessive gluttony, excessive drinking, excessive use of mind-altering substances, and excessive love for money and material possessions. By overdoing it, you not only waste the time you could have spent on other pleasures, but you also make your most powerful principles all the harder to find and achieve.

We can only learn through direct experience. One cannot be a painter without learning about colors, and how colors affect one's art. One cannot become a great cook or chef without knowing the flavors of food and how to create wonderful flavors. One cannot become a great writer without experiencing the wonder of words. This is true of every area of human endeavor and will be true of all human endeavor in the future as well.

We are all individuals with our own needs and agendas working together in groups. Individuals working alone or with others can come into conflict or turbulence for myriad reasons. It may be over a loved one, a parent's affection, a co-worker conflict, a parking space, or you name it. We have all seen and experienced turbulence, and cannot avoid the turbulence that inevitably comes into every life. Not only can we not avoid turbulence, we must learn to deal with it if we are to grow. Turbulence has a way of keeping us stuck in our relationships with others and hampers our ability to understand and accept ourselves.

The turbulence we encounter when connecting to the world and to the people around us often reflects turbulence within. This turbulence may be felt as a conflict of desires, a sense that desires are not being satisfied, a feeling that we are not able to reach a balance with what the world is expecting and what we can accommodate, or it can be a general feeling that we are not fitting into our world in a way that makes us comfortable. The way to internal balance, comfort with our values, and working with powerful principles is intertwined with the resolution of our internal turmoil. When an intention to resolve any feelings of internal imbalance is cultivated, we have an opportunity to find our powerful principles.

How you deal with turbulence and difficulties will determine both the quality and the direction of your life. Interactions between the outer and inner worlds can give rise to the emotions of turbulence, self-doubt, self-abuse, and loneliness. Invariably, this creates difficulties in our lives and with other people. Apt here is the old saying: "When you are upset, you kick the dog." One has to get to and through the places of turbulence and personal difficulty in order to get to the places of personal principled inclusion. Everybody goes through a version of this process, and the process is the same for everybody.

Our lives begin with and are defined by experience, and enjoyment in life depends upon how we relate to those experiences. Happiness depends on understanding, appreciating, and finding gratitude for our experiences. With this in mind, we can more quickly and safely return to a place of happiness when experiencing turmoil. The process of transforming turmoil will always involve calmness, compassion, and inclusion of self and others. Without calmness, internal balance can never be achieved nor can anyone arrive at the place of inclusion. Through this process we forge our principles, and those principles will help assure success, happiness, and effectiveness in the world.

The process of transforming turbulence is always the same with compassion and internal inclusion as essential elements of the process of transformation. Another essential ingredient is calmness because calmness breaks the spell of turbulence, and creates the spaces and time necessary to discover the feelings that drive the turbulence. Compassion helps clarify the feelings and calmness helps create the space for compassion to emerge. If we follow our own feelings into our inner core, we give ourselves a chance to find what we need.

WORKBOOK
Chapter Ten

1. Name ten things or qualities in your life that you are grateful for.

2. Can you see how you have learned to be grateful by the experiences you have had? Does this give you an idea about how you could learn to cultivate gratitude by expanding your experiences?

3. If you don't feel open to new experiences, can you identify any reasons why not?

4. Do you block the flow of gratitude? If so, how? Sitting quietly for a moment, can you see how gratitude comes to you by the way you are relating to the world around you?

5. Does inner turmoil play a role in your life? How does it manifest outside of yourself? Family? Friends? Work? Have you had inner turmoil in your life? Has it been a result of or connected with your relations with another?

6. How have you dealt with turmoil and turbulence in the past?

7. Are you open to ways to minimize or eliminate turmoil and turbulence in your life?

8. Are you willing to look within yourself to identify thinking and emotions that have contributed to the turmoil and turbulence you have had? Spend some time thinking and meditating on your connection to the turmoil, how you have felt about it, and what strengths and attributes you might get to start limiting and eliminating it.

9. Have you learned any methods of meditating or spiritual contemplation that you might use to deal with turmoil and turbulence? Have you been able to apply them in your daily life?

10. If you have not learned any methods of meditating or spiritual contemplation, are you willing to look for them?

11. If you have not sought nor found any forms of meditation or contemplation, are you willing to either look within yourself or ask others for help in confronting your personal turmoil and turbulence?

12. Recalling the chapter on Calmness in this book, is Calmness something you feel you are achieving in your life? Can you feel how it might help you? Are you willing to spend the time to search out the methods of accomplishing it?

11

THE NOW

The Now is a river composed of
an infinite number of Nows that make the river
all the more powerful and all the more compelling.

The importance of living in the Now cannot be overstated. Effectively engaging in the Now and being mindful of the world requires awareness, which requires calmness as an essential lesson on the path to mindfulness and self-reflection. We cannot achieve a healthy perspective of ourselves without calmness, and without it, we cannot experience compassion for self and others.

Without calmness, we are unable to focus our awareness due to the kinds of stress that manifest from internal conflict. Without calmness, we cannot resolve internal turbulence. As a way to think about our internal daily difficulties, we might compare them to the turbulence encountered on a river journey. The difficulties that spin us around and around and that cause confusion are similar to the turbulent vortex that blocks the flow of the river. That vortex and those blocks are capable of drowning us, and, for some, drowning turns out to be the reality.

Continuing the analogy of the river, we know that a single instance of the Now is not just one instance, but a rapid succession of infinitesimally small instances of the Now that flow like a river. We cannot really know all of the Now because so much of it is beyond human imagination and understanding. The many relationships and the equal number of influences that bear on the moment of our "Nows" often merge to create the reasons why our river of "Nows" is turbulent and difficult to navigate. How we navigate this river not only determines the depth and clarity of life experience, but also determines how much we can achieve. If we are stuck in our emotions, we will not easily escape the turbulence. If we cannot extricate ourselves from conflicts, we will not easily be able to enjoy life and will, instead, feel stuck and frustrated. When we are stuck, we are inclined to relate more to an exclusionary mentality, and not able to see the necessity of inclusion for the preservation of ourselves and life around us.

Without acting to escape the turbulence, the rushing of the river of Nows will only serve to increase the turbulence sucking us deeper and deeper into the dark water. The turbulence of one person, or one group of people, tends to attract more. Examples of this can be seen when one family member is in turmoil and the entire family gets pulled into the problem. It is often the case that one errant, violent person attracts violence to others with turbulent consequences lasting for years, decades, and even lifetimes.

Becoming aware of the elements that create turbulence is the beginning of a process that saves people from drowning. The development of our potential, and the full exploration of who we truly are, depends greatly on when and how we recognize turbulence, and how we begin and complete extrication.

The sources and contributors of turmoil and conflict can often be clearly identified. When that happens, it is relatively easy to direct attention to what is needed to make a thoughtful response. During a crisis or when a real threat is present, the fight or flight response and the necessary actions that follow from that response are quite clear. However, as the immediate threat dissipates, residual intrusive thoughts and emotional turmoil remain. If a trauma is deep enough, residual thoughts become contorted with long-term consequences. A vortex of turbulent feelings forms when residual consequences bind together. The turmoil we experience almost always begins at the intersection of our intentions and the intentions of others. No one can entirely avoid those tumultuous intersections and so finding ways to effectively handle those kinds of situations must be identified and introduced. Calmness is one time honored and clear way to handle turbulence and the resultant upheaval.

When we are calm, when we are contemplative, or when we seek in some way to alter how we sense the world, we change perspective and, therefore, often change the meaning of our lives. Our stress levels change for the better and with that, our health improves, and, frequently, we find a neutral feeling in the midst of turmoil. Being calm is crucial in finding that new perspective.

By stepping away from conflicts and difficulties, we achieve perspective along with the opportunity to see or observe our lives with clarity and insight. This is the best way to achieve self-understanding, self-awareness, and self-appreciation. Just as there are many schools and methods of meditation, there are many paths to the state of calmness including those found within various spiritual traditions or lineages.

In most spiritual traditions, calmness is an essential step and an important tool for self-discovery. If you want to improve your emotional quotient, and clarity of thinking, calmness is key. Without calmness as part of your daily routine, analytical skills suffer. Calmness is a necessary lesson needed to integrate the parts of yourself that form the basis of your principled inclusion with the world around you.

You can't expect to be involved with people without conflict because the basic nature of human beings includes conflict. You can't expect that all of your desires, wants, and needs will be free from doubt and inner turmoil. So often the many parts of our personality and character get confused or seem to be in conflict. How we organize our view of the world will depend, in great measure, on what we have encountered both as children and adults. Traumatic reactions are the most dramatic examples of disorganized views of the world, but there are so many other ways that we can have issues in making sense of the world because the world, with its turmoil, becomes part of us. It is in the search for our authentic, evolving self that we find our true and powerful principles. Calmness and compassion lead to personal inclusion and are essential steps in the search for our authentic selves.

With calmness you are able to bridge the gap between turmoil and integral personal inclusion. By distancing yourself from turmoil, you become aware of the people or elements involved in that turmoil and begin the ability to free yourself permanently from any persistent turbulence. Thought processes will help somewhat, but the most reliable way to get a handle on turbulence is through compassion.

Seek calmness first even in the midst of conflict. As a way to achieve a measure of calmness, allow yourself to not think about the situation at all. Everything you do in the name of calmness pays great dividends in terms of health and the search for identity. Calmness is an essential part of identifying with and working for the inclusion of all aspects of ourselves. Likewise, calmness is vital to the process of taking your integral self to the next level of powerful inclusion with the world. Principles are best forged and strengthened with calmness.

We generally think of compassion as being filled with sadness, pity, and sympathy along with the desire to alleviate the distress of another. That is not what is intended here. Empathy and compassion are sometimes used interchangeably. However, empathy has the additional connotation of somehow identifying with the emotions of another.

Compassion, as the word is being used here, acknowledges that, whatever the person did or continues to do that creates conflict, some level of emotion and feeling always accompanies that conflict. It is rare indeed to find momentous and conflicted issues that do not have substantial emotional aspects. Even if you can articulate logical reasons and explanations, thinking your way through these emotional aspects will often not be possible. Acknowledging and using compassion affirms the central importance that emotions have in continuing a conflict.

It is possible that letting go of unhealthy emotions will provide some measure of healing. Pretending that the turmoil will never return might also have benefits, but to truly resolve the issues, finding the places of emotional attachment in yourself will have more long-lasting benefits. Consciousness is the act of being aware of your emotions and searching for the attachments within yourself. Being conscious of our identity is a human trait that science, brain anatomy, and philosophy still find puzzling. Where does consciousness begin? How does it work? What does it mean?

Consciousness is personal and so varies from person to person. When in the grip of emotion, full or even partial consciousness about the emotion and its roots may not be possible. Lingering emotions are rooted in deep layers of ourselves. They may tie to our childhoods; they may well tie to some horrible trauma that we have been unable to address and still deeply fear.

When in the grip of intense emotion, being truly compassionate with yourself or others may be impossible. Being compassionate requires feeling the emotion, but not being overwhelmed by it. We cannot be fully present in the Now and we cannot be fully integrated if we are gripped by emotion. Being conscious of your emotions will always require gaining perspective. Perspective requires a vantage point, which will always require an imaginary positioning of the conscious mind in relation to the emotions. To position your conscious mind in relation to your emotions requires separation, self-observation, or the awareness of being aware of your emotions. It may be easy for you to separate from your emotions, but if not, a third person or counselor can help you discover that your emotions are meant to inform, not control.

There are also spiritual traditions and teachings that offer methods of separation from crippling emotions. Shamans do this by externalizing the emotion and dealing with it from a well-trained, safe distance. Christians often do this by placing their problems in the hands of their accepted savior. Buddhists do so through observation. Other religions have ways of dealing with unhealthy emotions as well. The field of Neuro Linguistics Programming (NLP) has pioneered ways to help achieve new ways of thinking with different perspectives to change a person's mindset.

It is in the fleeting moments of the Now that we are able to comprehend ourselves, and we truly swim in the river of Nows when we sense the illusion of time. Being in the river, makes us subject to the turbulence of the river. Our thoughts, emotions, feelings, and intuitions are all necessary for navigation. It is of little wonder that we all can feel, at least from time to time, an imbalance and a disconnection from ourselves. There is much that must come together to feel a sense of integrity. Using our senses, we create constructs that become the substance of our lives. What seems real is always changing. Therefore, the navigation of the river continues for as long as we are conscious. Give yourself the time and patience to get good at it. To the greatest extent possible, we must enjoy and savor our lives with both of those qualities being present throughout our lives from beginning to end. Gratitude and the enjoyment of life is key to our inclusion with ourselves, with others, and with the world.

WORKBOOK
Chapter Eleven

1. Have you practiced living in the Now? Can you see and feel how being aware of yourself and your surroundings is important to living in the Now?

2. Can you see how the present perceived moment of Now connects with those before and those yet to come? Can you take a few moments to sense how the Now moments connect like a river? Can you also sense how the energy in the river connects and drives all those moments?

3. Have you had the experience of chronic or repeated turmoil? When does that happen? Within family? Work relationships?

4. Imagine a life free of turbulence. What would that look like within and without?

5. How do you develop awareness, compassion, and calmness? What methods do you now practice? Are there others you would like to learn?

6. Have you thought about how calmness and compassion can incorporate the many parts of yourself? Are older ways of thinking about yourself interfering with your ability to do that? Can you see how the older ways have ignored your desires and needs? Can you see how those ignored desires and needs may be coming from aspects of yourself that you have not incorporated into your integrated self?

12

CONGRUENCE

If it's worth it, go for it!

Congruence is a state of agreement. It is a sense of fitting together in ways that feel right and make sense. People, ideas, and feelings that correspond and agree are considered congruent. Its opposite – incongruence – creates a feeling of imbalance, of not fitting together, of not agreeing. When something or someone seems fake, put-on, or even dishonest, they are considered to be incongruent as well. As an example, if you tell someone that you love them, while simultaneously frowning or grimacing, your profession of love will seem unbelievable, and, as a matter of fact, probably not true. Telling someone that you want to do something when you have deep-seated feelings against it, is incongruent. Desiring something that your religious teachings forbid is deeply incongruent. Taking part in a political or social action that you know is against your feelings or values is also incongruent. Anything that involves sensory or cognitive dissonance involves incongruity. To be less than congruent is to be less than fully committed to what is being expressed. It is dishonest to both give assistance to someone on one level and deny it on another. An example of a person or group behaving incongruently would be one that supposedly stands for something, but is doing something quite different when no one is looking. That sort of incongruent action is called hypocrisy, and because hypocrisy is a form of lying, it often has negative consequences. When we are not true to ourselves, we are misrepresenting who we are and that is also a form of lying. Whatever our personal foundation, it will be eroded by such misrepresentation or lies. A group that is built on lies will not have integrity. A personal life built on self-misrepresentation will likewise not have integrity. In other words, we have a great need to be as honest with ourselves as we can be. We can't have powerful principles, nor can we have authority and power with others if we have a misrepresented presentation of who we really are.

When we have thoughts or feelings that seem right for us at times, but we also have other contradicting thoughts and feelings, we are acting incongruently. When we say one thing, but think or feel another or even the opposite, we are incongruent, and, therefore, out of alignment with internal integrity. Actions based on incongruity do not emerge from internal integrity.

When we behave in ways that we know are wrong, those kinds of behaviors or actions are incongruent with who we are. Actions taken without heart or behaviors based in heartlessness should not be taken at all. When we act without heart, we are acting in a manner that is internally incongruent. Such actions do not have internal integrity, are not fulfilling, and often create more of the same in ourselves and others.

From time to time, we have all been dishonest with ourselves. Total honesty, in every situation, may actually be disruptive or hurtful if you or the people around you aren't prepared or capable of such honesty. Sometimes, other people really don't want to hear the whole story and would even be disturbed by it. For those reasons, everyone has engaged in "white lies" from time to time. We all must make decisions on what we say, and when and how we say it. We also have the right to base our actions on decisions that may or may not always have the hallmark of pure congruency or honesty. The consequences that result from any and all of our actions are always our responsibility. This is true as well in the Hindu traditions of India, which believe that we are all responsible for our own karma. Hindus believe that the actions we take will always have consequences with those actions creating and becoming part of who we are. What we create by our actions will define our fate and our destiny. More is discussed about karma in the notes of this chapter, but for now, suffice it to say that actions have consequences. Consequences are connected to our actions. Therefore, it is crucial to be ever conscious and aware of what we think, do, and say. Those thoughts, actions, and words will literally define who we are.

We cannot expect to have control in our lives unless we act in a principled manner. True principles always contain integrity and a high degree of interior congruence. We waste time – our own and everyone else's – when we engage in thinking and feeling in incongruent ways. We usually know that something is not congruent when it either does not make perfect sense, or when it just does not feel right. Congruence feels instinctual and correct.

If you have your heart set on something, but are offered something else, it would be incongruent to be effusively grateful for receiving it. At times, we have to act incongruently due to social constraints, but it does not give us satisfaction. An example of incongruent behavior that felt incorrect was when I was waiting on a street to see President Lyndon Johnson who was running for election after the death of John F. Kennedy. I was fifteen and waving my hand so that the president would see me. Johnson stopped and reached out his hand, but instead of shaking a hand or two, he merely grimaced and waved his hand above our hands. His hands were probably sore from touching too many hands, but the attempt to touch the hands and combine it with a grimace was most incongruent. It seemed like a lie, and to my fifteen-year-old sensibilities, I thought he must be very dishonest.

To be congruent in your interior life is to have thoughts and feelings that match in purpose, intensity, and quality. If you are thinking that something would be good for you, but your feelings about that "something" are weak, then take the time to discover why. If actions taken, based upon a thought or a feeling, do not achieve the desired result, or seem weak or in some way out of place, reconsider what you are doing. Perhaps they are not supported by strong and well-formed principles.

You will know when you are congruent in your interior life when you will feel comfortable with yourself. Congruence with yourself means that your competing parts are balanced in such a way that each receives the nourishment and attention needed for its existence. Interior congruence means that parts of your personality are able to move and vibrate smoothly and harmoniously within you. You'll know congruence when you feel it, and you'll feel it when you are congruent.

It may be difficult or elusive, at times, to reach internal congruence. Sometimes, it means that you have to confront parts of yourself that seem unfamiliar or that you have not wanted or been able to face. For most of us, there are aspects of ourselves that we have long ignored. Feelings of incongruence are a good indication that there is something or some part of you that you have ignored. When you are internally congruent, you can more easily and effectively confront and respond to conflict or turmoil, and you will be purposeful and directed in your response. When we are congruent, we possess strong, well-formed principles in a natural way. At a conscious and unconscious level, people respond more favorably and appropriately when we are congruent in what we say and do. Our unique and true voice comes from internal congruence based on strong principles. With strong principles, we act and speak in powerful and influential ways.

WORKBOOK

1. Have you had experiences either within yourself or in observing others of both congruence and incongruence? Reflect and write about each.

2. Can you sense how congruity is related to both truth and authenticity? Are there possibly incongruent thoughts, feelings, and desires that you have, which are detracting from your authenticity?

3. Can you see how incongruent actions can lead to distrust and conflict? Can you think of a time when your own incongruence lead to personal difficulty? Can you remember a time when you did not act on your best principles? Can you remember the incongruent feelings you had at the time?

4. Do you see examples of both qualities – congruence and incongruence – in public or world leaders? Do you believe that incongruent actions detract from the power and authority of leaders?

13

TURMOIL

Adversity provides opportunities
for understanding the world and ourselves.

There is an old expression "Don't look for trouble, it is looking for you." As much as we would like to avoid trouble, it has a way of happening. How we deal with trouble is a measure of our worth, and it is safe to say that trouble comes in many forms including inattention or misplaced attention. Trouble nearly always threatens an internal sense of comfort and balance. Serious trouble has the terrible consequence of separating ourselves from others. It gives us a sense of being "beside" ourselves and that we are not fully present. The integral self is always called to a connection with the outer world. The troubled self, however, remains in exclusion with the outer world because it is unhappy with itself.

When we have serious trouble, we can often have problems feeling our own integrity and, therefore, we cannot connect effectively or feel the outer world. As difficult as that may be to live with, the negativity and troubles of adversity can also serve a useful function because of the potential for teachable moments that result in self-integration and self-advancement. The more aware we become, and the more balance we achieve within ourselves, the more likely we are to discover or create principles that work. Whether we like it or not, our principles are determined by how we deal with adversity.

It is also true that the more balanced and aware we become, the more likely we will be to accept eccentricities or differences in others. In my early professional years, I was much less capable of accepting differences in others. Early success in my legal career lead me to believe that I was justified in an exclusionary view of others. Ignoring many of my internal needs and issues, I proceeded to validate my superiority, justifying why I was destined to walk over others to achieve a perfect, but isolated existence. Without a good sense of my own balance and without emphasizing my own integrity built upon my best principles, I allowed unscrupulous business partners to almost ruin my law practice and good name. There was no way to deal with those severe adverse events without looking into my core and returning to the principles that resonated with the values I knew to be true and correct for me. As I worked with my core principles and the parts of my own internal self, I began to have a much more balanced view of myself. Once that happened, it became natural to be less judgmental of myself and others. I began to see the virtue of the inclusion of others. I also began to see how my personal growth was at risk by excluding others from my life.

I learned that a balanced self is more inclusive both internally and externally. Strong principles emerge naturally and spontaneously when the balanced self is internally inclusive. Being shaken to my core was my way to find my core. Hopefully, there will be easier ways for you to find your core. The fact that you may not be shaken to your core does not make it any less important that you contemplate its importance. Your best principles come from that core and any principles you may adopt have less chance of serving you if they are in conflict with it.

If you have no turmoil and your life is all smooth sailing, then you won't as likely feel the need for examination of what you are doing or why you are doing it. For those lucky folks, it may still be recommended to do some self-examination to determine whether the stimulus and challenges of life are sufficient for self-development and personal growth. For most of us, there are always competing emotions and puzzling circumstances that leave us wondering, or even bewildered, as to what we should be doing, how we should be doing it, and what we should think about it. The turmoil that comes from this sort of bewilderment is internal. It likely has antecedents in how we developed, but has a current status of being an internal struggle of some sort.

How many people say they are not sure what they really want? How many folks do things that make them feel a little (or a lot) uncomfortable, but do them anyway? Many of our actions are habitual or derived from behavior we have acquired without critical analysis. In doing things routinely or from group pressure, it is possible that our inner needs are not being served. Our gut reaction or intuition tell us when something is not quite right. By listening to our inner voice, we can become more aware of our inner needs. Even though conventional and current thought discourages that kind of wisdom, we should allow ourselves the time to listen and respond to our inner voice. If something makes you uncomfortable or unhappy, stop, listen, and become aware of what your intuition and inner voice are saying. It will then be necessary to develop and practice discernment to determine if that inner voice is speaking from an integral and principled place of strength or one that is less developed and, therefore, weaker or even defective.

A strangled or suppressed inner voice produces a weak outer voice. Weak principles often come from those who suppress their inner voice and, therefore, their best character and personality. Any principles formed from such a suppressed inner self will naturally be weak, perverse, or oppressive. Even if they succeed in overpowering others, eventually, such principles and the people employing them prove to be hollow and ineffective. We have seen that in many of our nation's leaders. Richard Nixon, J. Edgar Hoover, and Joe McCarthy were men whose stated principles did not comport with their actions. We have to suspect that all three had an inner voice telling them to do something that was contradictory to what they were telling others. We also should suspect that all three did not achieve personal internal balance. The lesson we can learn from each of them is that we run the risk of being likewise discredited if we do not act in a manner consistent with our inner needs and our balanced self. An inner voice will tell you when you are doing things that are not resonant with your core values and your best principles.

While we should all strive to become adept at self-examination and self-acceptance, we must first calm any turmoil keeping us trapped. There is no shame, and only happiness, in discovering and addressing what may be causing inner turmoil. Of course, for some of us, there may be serious psychological conditions, horrible reactions to trauma or terror, and dangerous ideas and feelings of all sorts that require seeking and accepting outside help. If that is what it takes to heal and move forward in life, there is nothing wrong in doing this.

The necessary steps to calmness and compassion require addressing personal turmoil. Understanding ourselves and incorporating all the aspects of our lives and our personalities requires calmness and compassion. Personal inclusion in combination with inclusion of the world around us leads to greater happiness and more personal power.

While it is hard to be grateful for adversity, its importance for our development cannot be overstated. Turmoil and adversity can help to identify core values and point the way towards their use. As hard as it is to believe, turmoil is often the starting point for developing our core principles, and for that, we should be grateful for turmoil. Running from turmoil gets us nowhere. Confronting it with the intention of understanding turmoil and understanding ourselves gives us the opportunity to turn it into something positive for our own growth. The balanced self is the counter force to turmoil. To get to that balanced place always requires calmness and the equanimity of compassion. Frankly, once you know the emotional state of any opponent you have the key information to overcoming him or her. If you are unable to separate yourself from the emotional state of any person or group of persons, you will not be able to have the power to prevail. For this reason, your powerful principles must come from calmness and compassion. In this way they become truly your own.

WORKBOOK
Chapter Thirteen

1. Reflect on instances from daily life where turmoil has become chronic. How does that experience affect aspects of your life? What can you do to change? When you have had adversity, have you embraced it or did you run from it? Have instances of turmoil become chronic in your life? How has that turmoil affected your life? Reflecting on this, are there values and principles in your life that you can use to give you strength and purpose in confronting this turmoil?

2. Have there been times when you have needed outside assistance to address turbulence in your life or the lives of others? Where did you turn? Was it helpful in giving you a better understanding of your own inner-balance? Did that also lead to feeling more included in the world?

3. Can you find instances in your life where turmoil was useful in teaching you something about yourself? By confronting turmoil, were you able to be more compassionate with yourself, and with others too?

14

INTEGRITY

*Integrating yourself
with the world is the goal!*

Integrity is a quality that we all think we know and understand when we see it in others, but, at the same time, we may not be aware of in ourselves. True and powerful principles only come from a person with integrity and, by its definition, integrity only comes into being when a person is as unified as possible. The notion of being unified, however, should not be confused with uniformity. Integrity must be open to the diversity and complexity that is part of life. No one is totally uniform. You will find your integrity as a result of integrating disparate parts of yourself. Most of us are extraordinary in some ways, and most of us are complex in at least some ways. Notwithstanding our complexity and our internal differences, we still possess the capacity for integrity and our actions in life can always be based on that.

Principles that inspire effective and purposeful interaction with the world require that each person understands, accepts, and incorporates the totality of their thoughts and emotions in congruent and integrating ways. It means accepting with compassion the totality of who you are while knowing that the world will offer beings and situations that may be challenging at the same time. Once you have accepted yourself, it is much easier to include and accept what the world has to offer.

American Indians and other indigenous people understood this. Within the complexity and diversity of their spiritual traditions, one commonality was the idea of crossing various thresholds such as the passage to adulthood, which included finding a personal "vision" that supported appropriate interaction with the world. These ancient ways and traditions understood that effective interaction with the outside world required accepting both yourself and the spirit of those beings encountered and accepting that, within the inanimate world, spirits lived that must likewise be accepted and respected. Within these traditions, knowing that one can only be effective when one is responding with integrity to one's own vision is much the same as principled inclusion. Every man and woman must cultivate and sustain their life's private mission while incorporating themselves into the human community and the outside world.

Other spiritual traditions of the East and West similarly encourage the development of the individual while, simultaneously, encouraging acceptance and respect of the outside world. Buddhism and Sufism are two religious traditions that do this. Modern psychological practices and spiritual teachings such as Divine Science and Religious Science do so as well. All require personal development with inclusion of the world while discouraging exclusionary thinking. Without calling it "principled inclusion", that is exactly what is being taught alongside the understanding that we are in the world together, and neither we nor the world can effectively and safely exist until we connect the integrated self to the outer world.

Principled inclusion must come from a place of integrity and a deeply integrated self. When you have achieved congruence with the many varied aspects of yourself, you will know integration. Personal integration is always a movement toward personal integrity. The world cannot be powerfully encountered without personal integrity. For this reason, principled inclusion absolutely requires inclusion of all aspects of you. Just as the outer world must be accepted and respected, so must the inner world be accepted and respected.

Personal inner growth is never complete and is not intended to be. In each of our lives, there will always be a new challenge, a new aspect, changes that require adaptation, modification, creativity, and so forth. The outer world never stops presenting new challenges and the need for new responses or modifications of known responses emerge with each new challenge. Each new challenge requires a furthering or developing of perspective and, perhaps, a reevaluation of your principles. This requires both an inward search as well as a new outer response.

Perception and awareness are the key aspects that define successful personal inclusion as well as successful inclusion with the outer world. Personal perception and awareness all have their counterparts in lessons received from the outer world. Encounters with the outer world form the basis and provide references during the search for all aspects of you. The outer world informs and nourishes the inner world. The world that serves you and, in part, defines you exists in the air you breathe, the food you eat, the clothes you wear, and even the movies you have seen, music you have listened to and, of course, friends, family and others. Your inner nature and spirit have been formed and directed by all these influences and more.

If we are to achieve and sustain integrity, we must continually be sensitive and aware of our inner nature and what messages it is trying to send. Our values and principles come from those deep sources. Our true principles are not accidental, but rise from a life of mindful awareness and personal sensitivity. Integrity and powerful principles merge from these sources and are apparent to others in all the ways that we live.

WORKBOOK
Chapter Fourteen

1. Do you often feel that what you are doing does not fully express who you are? Are there activities you wish you could do, but have not been able to do? Do you feel there is anything holding you back from doing what you want to do? Do you feel this holds you back from having the integrity you would want to have? Can you list those things? Do you feel you can show this list to your friends, significant others, your family?

2. Do you have a vision of your future? If you are not happy with your present situation, can you conjure in your mind an idea of how you could start to change your life to something more satisfying? Can you spend some time thinking about it and writing it down? Do you have a friend, significant other, or family you can share this with?

3. List what you think your values and principles are that give you integrity. Is there anything holding you back from fully expressing them? Can you write them down? Can you write down some ways you could start expressing them more effectively?

4. Can you recall any time in your childhood where you felt that you were growing in your sense of yourself and how you fit into the world? As an adult, have you had any similar feelings? Can you describe ways that you presently express that growth you experienced? Can you write them down?

5. Once integrity has been developed, how can it be maintained? What challenges have you faced in life that have threatened your sense of integrity? Can you think of ways that you would like to grow in the rest of your life? Can you write them down? Can you imagine this might add to your integrity? Can you write down some of your thoughts?

15

EXCLUSIONARY THINKING

Focusing on the small keeps you small!

For much of human evolution, including the development of civilizations, the development of morality and propriety has both overtly and covertly depended on shunning, abandoning and, in some cases, destroying aspects of human beings considered abhorrent or unacceptable by dominant culture. From ancient through modern times, the destruction of an authentic self has been a fact of life for those with visions that do not include orthodox spiritual and religious tenets of the tribe, the city, the temple, the state, or any other controlling group. Those who have sought sexual expression in manners different from the dominant group or culture have likewise been punished and even tortured, while those who dress differently are mocked or ridiculed. From the days of branding a woman with a scarlet letter to the killing of homosexuals, which is still a regular occurrence in some parts of the world, we see the intensity of the kinds of violent punishments enacted against those who are different than the "norm". They are examples of how, throughout human history, oppression and isolation have been used to create the impression that such isolation and exclusion are essential for survival. Historically, perhaps, they have been used to assist in the survival of the tribe or nation, but that sort of survival mode is without value today. Exclusionary thinking threatens our growth and our survival.

Exclusionary thinking is also alive and well within our criminal laws and codes. In America, people can be incarcerated for decades and even for a lifetime. In many states such as Colorado, California, Florida, Tennessee, Virginia, Texas and so on, it is still legal to execute people. During the past three decades, prison industry growth in the United States has been exponential. The act of locking people up for decades can be considered a brutal form of exclusionary thinking. Many people feel satisfied by the argument that isolation is necessary for the safety of Americans. That may be true for a fraction of those who are imprisoned, but it is not true for the great majority who are imprisoned for non-violent offenses. An exaggerated sense of morality lies at the root of exclusionary thinking. It is a circular argument that lets exclusionary thinking justify itself. It is neither philosophically nor morally correct.

Whether or not any specific criminal law is justifiable, it is a fact that, in general, criminal laws are used punitively. In varying degrees of frequency, throughout the world, criminal laws exclude those who are judged as repugnant filling an increasing number of prisons with such people. In contrast, the ancient Chinese believed that prisons should be way stations where prisoners could be rehabilitated until it was possible to be returned or reincorporated back into society. Today, there are a few enlightened nations that follow that thinking, but they are not the majority.

Racial prejudice based on skin color or tone abounds and is another example of exclusionary thinking. Because of the color of their skin, people have been excluded and continue, in various ways, to be excluded from public life, from appropriate work, and from the free and welcome contribution of talents and skills. Certain groups are considered so repugnant that they are literally untouchable. Often, it seems as though dominant culture's continuity depends on the acts of exclusion of other groups. The argument always come down to a specious one: Our group won't exist without the exclusion of yours. Exclusionary thinking is the cause of untold cost, misery, and heartache.

In the United States, a nation built on the energy and creativity of generations of immigrant populations, the government periodically justifies the exclusion and banishment of immigrants. Untold numbers of immigrant populations have been working in America for decades, but exclusionary thinking would argue that they are "illegal" because their arrival in America was not by sanctioned means. They do not have "bona fides" to be included in American society. Even the children of immigrants, who have no choice in the act of immigrating, are excluded. Whether and how the enforcement of immigration laws is valid is not the issue. How difficult we make it for others to enter the country is also not the issue. Again and again, it is our old friend exclusionary thinking that is the issue.

Are some exclusionary methods acceptable, and if so how many? Perhaps an appropriate analogy is that of gardening. In a well-groomed garden, in order to cultivate certain plants, we need to weed out or exclude others. While some plants are perfectly beautiful as they are, they don't seem to belong within a cultivated garden. One solution has been to spray poison onto the less desirable plants. We know that poison in a garden leads not only to the death of the plants, but also to serious health problems for people and the rest of the environment. The same methods and underlying philosophy have been enacted in the control or eradication of insects. We know that the attempt to exclude insects from the environment in a garden or on a farm or even in a jungle has led to the die-off of all manner of insects. Because of the inter-connectedness of all species, killing off insects has led to the unexpected killing off of a general quality of life on Earth. We need look no further than the endangerment of bees and monarch butterflies and the ways that their eradication positions other species, including the human species, for eradication as well.

Orderly and principled inclusion of all of the Earth's life should be our goal, with a few exceptions such as viruses. The AIDS virus, smallpox, and poliovirus are three examples of certain viruses that appear to be of no benefit other than to benefit their own life cycles. It is possible that we will discover that even that understanding is not entirely true, but for the time being, we are constrained to order their total exclusion.

Exclusionary thinking, whatever its immediate justifications, always carries the risk of affecting our ability to include the outer world within

ourselves. We must develop methods of widespread and accepted principled inclusion if our species and all who have evolved alongside us are
not to be doomed. Our attitudes and behaviors are threatening to do
irreparable damage to the Earth's biosphere. Respect for life should be the
basis for human morality and ethics.

Can we all agree all of the time on the proper principles of inclusion?
Probably not, but we will be lost if we cannot agree that we must include
all of life and the many varied principles of others in our worlds. The best
we may be able to hope for now is that more people will start questioning
exclusionary thinking and insisting on ways and methods that embrace
rather than exclude. When confronted with exclusionary thinking we
must always insist on its current cost and its long-term effects.

WORKBOOK
Chapter Fifteen

1. Are you a member of any group that practices exclusion of others? Does your church exclude any people, or are they embracing of others? Do you see the benefits of including others and the detriment of excluding others? Are there ways they could reasonably be more inclusive? Can you write down your thoughts on this?

2. Can you share those thoughts with others?

3. Write down your thoughts about how exclusionary thinking affects:

   • Legal systems?

   • Racial bias?

   • Sexual expression?

4. What are the connections between personal inclusionary thinking and the same extended into the public or political realms? Can you imagine the benefits that might come to you by being more inclusive of the world around you? Can you imagine a world that is more inclusionary? Can you write down and share your ideas with others who are important in your life?

5. Write down how inclusionary thinking might be of benefit to you, your family and friends. If your friends might not be supportive, write down the reasons why not. Ask yourself if you could share this with those friends, or whether you should try to share those thoughts with another group of people. If your present circle would likely not be supportive of your thoughts of inclusion, write down what you think you would gain by finding people who would be supportive.

16

SUCCESS
AND DIRECTION

Fine-tuning and how to do it.

Success happens when you have a sense of direction. Success happens when you know what you want. Success happens when you know what you need. Success happens when you know how to find the assets and resources necessary to get what you want and need. It may be true enough that you don't need any sense of direction, consciousness, assets, or resources and, instead, will be simply lucky enough to achieve success by blunder, but don't count on it. Or don't count on it happening more than once.

Success is always relative and dependent on the definition of an individual or group. Let's imagine that your version of success is defined as walking to the corner. How can you describe what is needed in terms of assets and resources required to do that? First, you need the desire to arrive at the corner along with the physical capacity to walk, which includes the ability to move your legs. Next, you'll need to know the corner's location and either already have or develop the necessary skills to see, feel, or find your way there. You might also think about why you want to go to the corner in the first place. What will you do when you get there? How long will you stay? When is a good time to leave the corner? Where will you go? If you are reasonably fit, getting to the corner might be no big deal, but if you have COPD, getting to the corner is a worthy goal and arriving there a great achievement. How will you feel about a successful mission to the corner? Can you imagine a celebratory party?

This sequence or series of questions and requirements for "getting to the corner" is the same for everything you do and everything you seek to achieve: 1. Understand the goal or outcome; 2. Assess resources and how they will be used to achieve the goal; 3. Contemplate the outcome as well as any consequences, and remember that while it is possible to consider the consequences without consideration of the impact, you do so at your own peril and the peril of others.

As we go along in life, we consciously or unconsciously develop awareness of its unfolding direction. From time to time, when things seem out of place or heading the wrong way, we are called to change direction correcting our course. There are times in life when its direction is the result of expediency without adherence to any values other than immediate reward. It is always our responsibility to sense the direction of our lives paying attention so that the direction always correlates to the values we hold. Maintaining the foundation of these life values is our own responsibility. Ignoring the foundation may allow it to erode. We risk our integrity to say or do something just because it is easy or profitable unless it fits with who we are and what we believe. Our foundation is part of our integrity, and depends on being aware of how all of our parts fit together. Stay aware of who you are and don't sell yourself short by doing something for expediency only.

Always remember that while relationships, achievements, and resources may belong to you for a time, and may even define you in your own mind and in the minds of others, they are not you. Not really. You are much grander and more than the sum of those parts. The elements at the basis of who you are – your foundational elements and essence – are key for inclusion, first and fundamentally to yourself, and then to the greater world. Until you connect to your version of inclusion, you will not be able to effectively, efficiently, and powerfully connect to the greater biosphere or outer world. Remember this idea from Chapter Two of this book: "Inclusion blends two paths: one inward and one outward." And these from Chapter Three: "True values and true principles must emerge from an inner understanding, a balanced internal sense of self, and an elementary personal integrity. Understanding, internal balance, and integrity are not just worthy goals, but essential attributes for anyone who wants to develop powerful principles."

The maintenance of a sound and vital foundation requires objectivity, awareness, and perspective. That cannot be overstated. Your foundation is the basis of your integrity and it will be the place, figuratively speaking, where your principles are forged and where the reappraisal of your principles should be performed when necessary. No book or manual can describe your foundation or how to understand, repair, or modify it when necessary. When and if your values or your principles are called into question, damage can be done to the stability of your foundation. Any serious affront to your integrity reverberates to the core of your foundation and principles. Discord and turmoil in life create a feeling of imbalance and dislocation. With an awareness of personal integrity and primary principles, you are better able to recognize the worth of your values and how to use your principles to guide your direction in life.

When the forward movement of life has slowed or stopped through the influence or actions of others, it is a good idea to review your values and principles. Ask yourself if your core, fundamental values are worthy. Are they still working in harmony with your inner self even if others get in the way or fail to understand and provide support? Review your principles as they apply to the issues and personalities at hand. If modification seems in order, do so. If not, rest on your principles realizing that to do so is to reinforce your integrity from which your calmness and balance will emerge. When everything is going our way and our principles and our methods are working for us, we have no reason to question our principles. However, when we must forcefully assert our values, when our principles cause or extend a conflict, we should ask ourselves if, fundamentally, we need to make changes or whether we should double down and dig in with the principles we have been using. This what it takes to live an examined life. Difficulties frequently cause some to shut down, feeling powerless with their own principles. Dysfunction displayed around us may cause us to feel "beside ourselves" or not entitled to connect to ourselves. Those times, more than others, are when we need to find the fortitude to look inward toward our core values and strong principles.

It is a universal human desire to be successful. The fact is that you become somebody when you are somebody. It is the somebody you are to yourself that radiates and includes others achieving what you have sought with the integrity of your heart and mind. If it happens haphazardly, or as the result of a quick grab, success may be either elusive or short-lived. If you are looking for money, let it chase you, don't try to run it down. Likewise, if you need direction, don't try to chase after something, rather find the direction in your heart, intuition and best thoughts. If you need help in organizing your thoughts, to quiet down too many thoughts, or to soothe something in your heart, don't be embarrassed to ask for it. Remember that it is you who should create and follow your direction, not someone else.

WORKBOOK

Chapter Sixteen

1. How do you define success? What is your version of "getting to the corner"? Can you see that success is often relative to the moment? Can you see that success is relative to who is judging it? Can you remember times when you succeeded and how people reacted? Can you remember any times when you thought you succeeded, but others either did not recognize it or did not appreciate how important it was to you? What do you think are the differences? How should your success be judged and by whom?

2. Have you experienced success? What do you think your mental state was when you were doing the activities that were rated as successful?

3. Have you had the experience of chronic or repeated turmoil that lead to lack of success? When does that happen most often? Within family? Work relationships? Can you identify anything that keeps you bound up in that turmoil? Can you think of anything you have read in this book that would let you start disengaging from that turmoil?

4. If you have not had the success you have wanted, are you ready to reassess your goals and your projected outcomes? Are you ready to reappraise your principles to see if they are adequate to the challenge or whether you need to start to apply principles you already have?

5. Can you see that your success will depend upon your own internal sense of direction? Can you see any need to change your own internal direction, or do you need to increase your efforts for the direction you are going? What would you like to achieve? What principles would you apply and what resources will you need? Does this make your success more likely?

17

EXISTENTIAL CRISES
AT THE CROSSROADS
OF LIFE ON EARTH

*A call to inclusive action
for the good of all!*

Our modern world and, especially, the worlds of the 20th and 21st centuries have presented us with, at least, five existential crises including:

- The crisis of dysfunctional human interaction manifesting in violence, human isolation and loneliness, terrorism, and more.
- The crisis of an epidemic of people suffering from a fractured sense of self, a sense of emptiness, and a sense of inner discord manifesting in anxiety, depression, severe personality and psychological disorders, and addiction.
- The crisis of spirit or soul felt in the absence of a sensible relation with the transcendent spirit called God or the Great Spirit.
- The environmental crisis or breakdown of the material world and all living beings manifesting as a disconnection and extinction of thousands of living species.
- The evolving and devastating crisis of robot or machine culture manifesting as the automation of work (putting human beings out of work) and the dominance of artificial intelligence.

Disconnection is at the core of each of these existential crises. Each has the element of exclusion rather than inclusion. Each involves isolation or separation containing as well a fear of being alone. Each features an unwillingness to share or the evidence of the "consciousness of scarcity" rather than the feeling of abundance and plenty for all.

Fundamentally, each exhibits the lack of elemental integrity, and that we are fractured in ourselves and isolated from others. This absence of connection to the whole, or to greater good, appears on the individual level as well as within large and small groups, communities or regions, and in the great nations of the world. Those who yearn for a spiritual connection to others, to the Earth, and to the Great Creator sense this disconnection and feel despair. Those who understand deeply that humans are connected to and dependent upon every other species on Earth seek ways to stop the extinction by the works and hands of humans before it is too late if it isn't already.

The disconnection is clear. The failures caused by disconnection are clear. The discord and violence caused by disconnected groups, tribes, and nations is clear. The serious divide of political parties is clear. The spiritual disconnection felt by so many is palpably evident. There is a vast number of sad descriptions of the emotional toll of the loneliness of the modern isolated life. Individual lives and the lives of other species are affected by this isolation and exclusion. The vast fabric that connects us to one another as individuals or as parts of groups and species has unraveled. This is true as well with the experiences of the long-term unemployed, those imprisoned, those suffering food shortage, and those living behind gates and walls. All are living excluded lives.

Rather than dwell on the disconnection, look to its opposite. Look to inclusion. Look to the ways that each individual can connect. Look to the ways we can include various peoples, tribes, communities, and nations of the world. Look to the ways we can find an innate spiritual and transcendent connection to others and to the Great Creator. Last, but not least, look to the ways we can make connections to the teeming life of the Earth and to the elementary thought that started and maintains the basis of all life, which is the DNA that supports all of thought on the Earth.

Through understanding and applying the fundamental principles of inclusion, we will make the connections needed to survive as a species and as a planet. Principled inclusion presumes that there is a structure and a method for looking within, acknowledging the conscious and the unconscious, the obscure and the obvious, strengths and weaknesses, voids and empty spaces, and accepting and connecting all with compassion to the outer world. If we make use of the guiding principles of inclusion, we have the greatest chance of finding answers to our existential crises.

Inclusion can also be found within the realm known by the great majority of humans as the realm of spirit. In that realm, there are many who reach beyond "regular" life to find answers from a transcendent source, or who have experienced inclusion with a transcendent reality. For those folks, it is a transcendent power that offers support and their world is mediated by that power. Their sense of inner and outer connection presupposes and relies on the transcendent power, and any principled inclusion with the world requires that transcendent power. These connections are essential for those who are called believers, and their methods are easily incorporated in the methods of principled inclusion.

When we are seeking answers to the dilemmas and turmoil in our lives, it is essential to look for answers beyond our usual understanding. Using your integrity, internal sense, and best judgment, be open to answers no matter their origin. Seek the answers in your dreams, and let your spirit take you where answers can be found. For this purpose, it may be best to dispense with your fear and judgment of the "source" of the answer. Let yourself be the judge of whether it fits. If it fits, wear it. If it does not involve the reasonable inclusion of the broad world around you, be sure you have asked as many questions as you can as to why or why not. Keep asking those questions as you keep developing the powerful principles of inclusion. Your success and the success of the world depend on it.

If you have ever felt the exhilarating feeling and the joy of inclusion, you can understand that inclusion brings energy and a purpose that was absent before the inclusion. Inclusion with principles and purpose not only bring joy and exhilaration, but more lasting and satisfying connections. In other words, if you bring the principles of your own

WORKBOOK
Chapter Seventeen

1. Write a letter to yourself describing what good you could bring to others around you. Write a letter from your heart to the most important person in your life whether they are alive or deceased. Remind yourself of the love you may have found in your life and see if you can direct some of that now to yourself.

2. Remember how good it felt to be included by your family, by your work, by a significant other, or maybe even by a stranger. How might you be able to do that for others in your life?

3. Use your imagination and write at least a paragraph or two about how the world would be improved if most people practiced inclusion.

4. Write a paragraph or two about how your own life might improve if you could include more people in your own sphere. Maybe your ideal life includes money, food, or affection, but let your imagination guide your writing as if no one will see what you have written. After all, it is from your imagination. Remember dreams do come true!

18

CONCLUSION

*Never be embarrassed to act as if you are important,
and to seek greatness in yourself and others!
You have every right to be influential, effective, and powerful!*

Exclusionary thinking always involves limitations. Atavistic thinking, such as tribal thinking, harkens back to earlier eras when protection from outside dangers was paramount. Growth in civilizations documents the growth of principled individuals acting on their principles, who included more of the world through exploration, innovation, discovery, spiritual development or other activities that advanced human understanding and experience.

Human endeavor and achievement are impossible to explain or understand without mentioning those who acted on principle and sought inclusion and were, therefore, seminal in the development of human civilizations. In that list we might include: Susan B. Anthony, the Buddha Siddhartha Gautama, Julius Caesar, Jesus Christ, Christopher Columbus, Thomas Edison, Albert Einstein, Mohandas Gandhi, Helen Keller, Martin Luther King, Marco Polo, Eleanor Roosevelt, Nikola Tesla, Harriet Tubman, George Washington and so many other innovators and leaders. All share strong and abiding principles that directed their actions combined with the essential ingredient of seeking to include and advance the interests of others. All of these leaders, explorers, and innovators dedicated their lives and actions to their principles, and because of that, changed the course of human history.

The power of principled inclusion is not the purview of superb leaders only, but is central to any successful endeavor within families, businesses, and nations. Often, the success of any endeavor is due to principled people working together. Nations, businesses, schools and universities have been formed and founded by individuals acting in concert for the common good.

Human success is dependent on individuals with identifiable principles acting congruently and with integrity to extend improvement of others or the environment through the principles of inclusion. The essential integrity found within each leader is an awareness of themselves in tandem with those they wish to accommodate or connect to their activities. Successful human activity almost always affects and connects with others far outside the immediate circle of the primary actors and actions reverberating for millennia.

Most certainly, the challenges faced by the human race and much of life on Earth require that people of principle band together to work inclusively in solving current problems that now threaten the life of the planet. Exclusionary thinking has no place in the race to solve the problems confronting our species and every species. The goal is to reach ever greater inclusion. We find our own internal growth and our own internal connections by finding and nurturing our integrity. What we give always returns. Let us not forget to live in gratitude, and to have the compassion that is essential for health. Work to develop Calmness while awakening awareness and keeping awareness active.

Inclusion with yourself and as much of the world as you can reach is always the goal. Find your principles and do not stray from them any more than you absolutely have to. If, over the course of your life, you find that your principles need modification, amend them. Every breath of every day is important, so remember to breathe. You have every right to be influential, effective and powerful!

NOTES

Chapter 1:
The Foundation of All Principles

Theories about child learning almost always deal with the *how* of learning and not the *why* of learning. Why are children curious? What is it that makes a child want to continually experiment and play with its world? Is natural curiosity something that inevitably wanes in most children, or is there something about learning that causes it to wither? Curiosity involves the joy of exploration. Perhaps, if we understood more about why children are curious, we would be able to tailor education in ways that would allow curiosity to continue or even to thrive as education proceeds.

If one uses a simple definition of genius – that a genius is one who discovers something unique that others have not theretofore discovered – then even the average child is a genius. Through a process of self-discovery, children continually find ways to either create new things or to bring about new combinations of things.

The word "education" comes from the old Latin meaning "to lead out of". Even the word for the process of education provides an understanding that education attempts to put the educators' stamp on how and what the child learns. Inevitably, this results in a loss of the child's ability to take initiative or bring the quality of innovation to the act of learning. Genius does not involve mimicry, but rather seeing things in a new light. Being a genius is not always easy, but is always original and calls for a unique combination of thought and emotion individual to each genius. As we find our own integrity and our own paths, we are required, in a way, to assume the role of a genius for ourselves. We must find the novel path that suits us.

Gratitude is more than simply feeling grateful. We cannot be grateful for what we do not know. I received inspiration for what I now know as the "Realm of Gratitude" and wrote extensively about it in my first book, *Turbulence in the River*. In that book, that received inspiration taught me to ". . . take all that is good and all that is supporting and put it around you to facilitate the open feeling of warm embrace that is Gratitude, but do not seek to win those resources in your Gratitude. Rather, know that those resources and supporting things are yours in abundance, many more than you know or can ever hold or count."

In that first book, *Turbulence in the River*, I wrote about how gratitude allows our hearts to open as large as possible. If we open ourselves to the full experience of the world, we can dispel any feelings of inadequacy. We put the ego to the side so that it does not constantly direct us, which helps us get rid of any feeling of a failed self. Also, we are less apt to pass judgment on what is good or bad when we see the full array of possibilities available. In my book, I wrote: "Gratitude is content to encounter the universe. No matter what happens, with Gratitude one knows that all is okay in the connection with the universe" and ". . . living in the Realm of Gratitude requires living in the "is" of Now. The "is" takes in all the past and future. The nuances of experience are what change both the past and the future. The past is changed in its effect on the "is" of Now, when we change the nuances of it, and likewise the future is changed when we change the nuances of what we expect, see, and feel about the future. Practicing living in the "is" of Now will serve to expand your feeling of Now."

Values –

We use the word expecting that everyone knows what it means. Wikipedia states: "In ethics, value denotes the degree of importance of some thing or action, with the aim of determining what actions are best to do or what way is best to live, or to describe the significance of different actions." The Oxford Dictionaries defines "value" as "Principles or standards of behavior, one's judgment of what is important in life."

Neuro Linguistic Programming (NLP) uses the concept of "values" to indicate the "why" of what a person does. For more information on NLP see: *Thorson's Principles of NLP* (1996) by Joseph O'Connor and Ian McDermott; and *Principles of NLP* (2013) by the same authors.

Values are not the same as principles. Values are much more central to a person's life and less subject to change than principles. Principles are your distilled reasons for doing what you do, and these may change or be modified by the reaction you receive when using them. Principles should be consistent with values, but they are not the same as values.

Dr. Ed Diener is a University of Illinois psychology professor and a pioneer of research on the topic of happiness. In *Happiness: The Science of Subjective Well-being* (2008) co-written by Diener and his son Robert Biswas-Diener, the state of happiness is defined as a "non-logical, subjective sense of well-being" with the five elements of happiness including: positive emotion, engagement in life, meaning, positive relationships, and accomplishment. Other psychologists have identified two parts of happiness: Eudaimonic happiness and Hedonic happiness. Eudaimonic happiness identifies well-being as something arising from having purpose and of being in service to others. Hedonic happiness comes from the feeling of pleasure.

Dr. Sonja Lyubomirsky is a professor of psychology at the University of California, Riverside who authored the book *The How of Happiness*. She recommends practicing gratitude as a powerful activity from which to experience happiness. Lyubomirsky writes: "Happiness does not come only from doing pleasant things" (Lyubomirsky).

Often happiness comes from doing well at less than pleasant things. The Roman poet and philosopher Titus Lucretius Carus (known as Lucretius) wrote: "Ut quod ali cibus est aliis fuat acre venenum" (what is food for one man may be bitter poison to others) in the first century BC.

Happiness certainly must come from our experiences. As discussed in *Turbulence in the River*, the Realm of Gratitude is the realm of all our experience because it is the universe around us that contains happiness, sadness, joy, and strife. What you get out of it depends on what you put into it. Can someone be happy when they are unemployed? An increasing number of people really have no choice in either being unemployed or working at a job that gives them much less than they want or deserve. Can an injured or sick person be happy? Again, some folks have no choice. Are they all to be denied happiness? The hope is that no one should be denied happiness.

The word "meta" is defined as transcending, encompassing or pertaining to a level above or beyond. Metadata for instance is data that describes data. Metalanguage is language that describes language. I have used the term "meta-observation" to mean observing something from a level above, a distant level, and a level from a different perception.

This is related to the NLP use of perceptual positions. NLP defines five perceptual positions:

- 1st position is seeing or feeling from our own standpoint.
- 2nd position imagines from another person's standpoint.
- 3rd position is an *independent observer* watching interaction between positions 1 and 2. It is an outside point of view.
- 4th position observes the third position watching the independent observer.
- 5th position is further removed, observing yourself as an observer.

The first position is the usual position that humans take. The second through the fifth positions provide us with the meta-view – a view above or beyond – that takes us out of a position in which we may be stuck or where we may lack a full perception of whatever thing or process we are observing. It increases our abilities of observation.

Perceptual positions allow us to have perspectives we would not otherwise be able to achieve. One can certainly say it only involves the imagination, but, by imagining, we see and feel things differently, thereby setting new programs for ourselves. These methods get better with practice. Start working with them and, when you are confronted with anything disconcerting, use the perceptual positions to remove yourself to a place of calmness. Meditation and silence are also very useful. The more time you spend with these calming techniques, the better you will be with rising above conflict, finding your compassion, and achieving inclusion. It is all part of the process of finding your internal balance and your spiritual connections.

Knowing your resources, how to access, use, and appreciate them is an important concept in applied Neuro Linguistic Programming (NLP). One tenet of NLP is that change comes when there are positive, identifiable outcomes for each person practicing NLP.

Outcomes may vary: one may be to become more effective with people; one may be in losing weight or becoming more physically fit; other outcomes may be finding more cooperation, more attention, and even more love. Whatever the outcome, a person needs to identify the positive steps to get there, the resources needed, and the possible consequences that will result when the outcome is achieved. Throughout the process of achieving an outcome, your core principles will be the guiding lights. My spin on NLP is that principles are key to the whole process of effective internal balance and effective interaction with the world. See *Core Transformation: Reaching the Wellspring Within* (1994) by Connirae and Tamara Andreas.

Positive attitudes, positive outcomes, and positive emotions are important and represent the difference between "I don't think I can" or "I don't want to" and "I want it" and "I know I can get it" and "I will find the resources to get it." Much about our lives is not positive, but is distinctly negative. Is the negative to be avoided or it is to be embraced?

In *Turbulence in the River*, I wrote: "The negative involves a lesson of something in need of fulfillment or in need of completion. It is part of the circle that needs to be closed with the addition of something yet unknown to the conscious of the present moment."

I learned about the uses of the negative when exploring the teachings revealed to me over a four-year period and that I, subsequently, revealed to a larger public in *Turbulence in the River*. I learned that negative thoughts, feelings, and actions are stuck patterns that we cannot escape, but must cherish as part of who we are. They are a resource that the attitude of Gratitude would have us embrace. We must seek the completion of the negative. It demands that we find the complementary part that fits the template of the negative and gives it completion. The complementary part of the negative is indeed the positive to which we should be directed. To stay in the negative is a grave mistake; we must be open to its lessons.

Chapter 2:
The Two Paths of Inclusion

The unconscious mind is an important concept in modern psychology and psychiatry. Although it did not originate with Sigmund Freud, his theories and his writings in psychiatry became so popular and pervasive that he is given credit for "discovering" the unconscious mind. Freud postulated that there are three levels of the mind: conscious, preconscious, and unconscious. He connected those levels to what he said are three levels of the mind: the Ego, the Id, and the Superego. The Id is the primitive and instinctual part of the mind to which Freud attributed sexual and aggressive human drives. The Superego is the moral consciousness, and the Ego is the realistic part of life that operates between the Superego and the Id. Freud believed that the Id was infantile, unaffected by logic or reality, and did not change during one's lifetime.

In 1900, Freud published *The Interpretation of Dreams* stating that dreams are the "Royal Road to the Unconscious". He believed that dreams reveal suppressed or hidden feelings and thoughts, and that most repressed feelings were sexual in nature. Modern day psychiatry and psychoanalysis has moved beyond this limited view, but the concept of the unconscious is solidly accepted in modern medicine, psychology, and neuroscience.

Carl Jung, a protégé of Freud's, developed his own concepts of the unconscious mind. For Jung there were three main levels of the mind: the Ego, the personal unconscious, and the collective unconscious. In Jungian psychology, the Ego processes our thoughts, memories, and emotions. The unconscious in Jungian psychology has its differences, but for superficial analysis the power and extent of it is similar. Jung's theories of the "collective unconscious" differ completely from Freud's, and have not been uniformly accepted in psychology or psychiatry. He believed that the human mind contains innate characteristics that are the results of our evolution and our ancestral past. Jung postulated that our ancestral memories become "archetypes" which are shared throughout different human cultures. One archetype is the "persona" or the public face we present to the world. Another is the anima/animus which presents male and female aspects to the world. Another is the "shadow" or animal side of our nature and another is the "self" which is the part of us that gives us our individuality. Jung believed that men and women share both male and female aspects. He believed that our "self' is in conflict with our primitive instincts. Jung was clearly mystical and admitted being influenced by what he saw as psychic powers. He originated the concept of two character types: extroversion and introversion. He also identified the four basic human psychological functions: thinking, feeling, sensing, and intuiting. By combining the four human characteristics with the two character types, Jung discovered eight personality types. He believed in the great universal meaning of legends and myths, and that our deep psychological thoughts often transcend the individual and are shared by others. His writings are fascinating and deeply provoking.

Neuroscience has identified many brain functions that create in us a sense of self. Some are in the older and deeper part of the brain and some are in the more advanced cerebral cortex of the brain. Psychology, philosophy, and neuroscience all deal with the ideas of self, interaction with the world, and internal balance. Often the ideas intersect to support each other. Often it seems they are referring to different things. For purposes of personal development and the implementation of your own principles, read and think about the various theories and studies because they will support your pursuit of your core, your values, and your principles that let you express yourself to yourself.

Chapter 3:
Controlling Personal Destiny with Personal Principles

Personal authenticity is a popular concept that expresses a widely held view that we are compelled to be as true to our own selves as we can be. This is not a new concept. As long ago as 1599, in "Hamlet", Act 1, Scene 3, William Shakespeare wrote: "To thine own self be true."

Making personal authenticity a goal is as much a matter of ethics and morality as it is psychological and spiritual truth. For some thinkers, including Simon Feldman, the author of *Against Authenticity, Why You Shouldn't Be Yourself* (2014), the idea of authenticity is suspicious as if "self-love" is the same as "selfishness." One has only to Google "popular books on authenticity" to find a large number of good books that deal with the idea of self-acceptance, personal creativity, self-compassion, as well as the courage to own your own beliefs.

From my personal view, the concept of authenticity has a connotation of being restrictive and even a bit sanctimonious. I prefer the word "real". Your real self is who you are and needs no certification of authenticity or proof as it appears so to others. Your real self may seem to be so much like thousands of others that you cannot be found in a crowd. Your real self may be self-effacing and it may have no self-love at all. However, if all that is what seems the most real and internally consistent to you, then who is to judge? If it does not really feel like you, then seek the answers on how to find the real you.

Emotional balance is known in psychology to occur when we are able to experience our emotions without being overwhelmed or unduly stifled by them. Many writers express these ideas. One good example is *Emotional Balance* (2011) by Dr. Roy Martina.

Emotional balance assumes some ability to understand and work with our emotional selves. Emotional intelligence (EQ) is a fairly new concept for which there is no current agreement among psychologists. EQ requires an awareness of emotions (of yourself and others), an ability to access your own emotions, and an ability to manage those emotions. These are all "squishy" concepts that fall under the category of "we know it when we see it". The tests for emotional intelligence are all contextual, and mostly subjective. David Goleman's book, *Emotional Intelligence* (1995), is highly recommended as a way to understand various aspects of EQ or emotional intelligence and how it is conceptualized.

Mind control is an extreme form of influence and persuasion thought to disrupt a person's sense of identification, and a way of controlling the thoughts and actions of another. Mind control – also called "brain washing" – manipulates and changes attitudes, beliefs, and behavior. In *Cults in Our Midst* (1996), Margaret Singer discusses a six-point system describing the process of mind control saying: "The person is unaware that there is a system controlling them, their time and environment is controlled, they are made to be fearful and dependent, their previous behaviors and attitudes are repressed, new behaviors and attitudes are installed and they are presented with a doctrine that has closed logic." Mind control occurs in political movements, strict schools, companies that control the thoughts of their employees, military units, and more. There can even be one-on-one cults in the case of an abusive spouse or parent. When any thought becomes knee-jerk, impulsive, or lacking in individual analysis, we must be suspicious that these thoughts are being controlled by others (even relatives or leaders who may be deceased.)

A person experiences mind control when they feel compelled to look for direction from another, or feel as if they don't have resources upon which to rely, or feel inadequate doubting an internal balance while being subjected to an outside influence that both offers a solution and insists it must be done with the influence and help of one (or a group) asserting control. An ever-present aspect of mind control is the notion that, only in the exclusive group or relationship, is there an acceptable situation. There have been a number of "self-help" or "self-betterment" groups in recent history that have outwardly sold the idea of individual strength and individual betterment while, in reality, promoting an ideology and belief system that required loyalty to group norms and group hierarchy.

Adherence to anyone else's rules must be suspect if it leads to membership (group inclusion) in something that is unduly or unnecessarily exclusive. Membership in a union may be acceptable, for instance, because of its likely necessity to protect labor rights. Membership in a fraternity might also be acceptable given the benefits of membership. Membership in a fraternity that requires separation from other relationships might not be worthwhile. The issue at hand must always be the protection of one's own judgment, independence, and integrity. Admittedly, there will always be the need for balance, but critical analysis and independent judgment skills must be included within that balance.

Codependency is a concept that first began to be understood in Al Anon, the support side of Alcoholics Anonymous. The term has been used to describe a person who compulsively attempts to control while being unable to control a relationship with a chemically dependent person. The term has grown in acceptance to include relationships where one or both partners are obsessive, controlling, and self-destructive. There may or may not be obvious abuse. Relationships like these are always out of balance, and never allow for individual independence and expression. The term is not meant to include couples who rely on each other for emotional and physical support, even if it is, at times, intense and unusually strong. The term is meant to describe relationships that are dysfunctional, and where neither partner experiences satisfaction.

It is not clear when or where the idea of setting "healthy" boundaries in personal relationships first entered the fields of psychology and pop-psychology. The concept, of course, is one that originated with descriptions of land, but has become ubiquitous in describing how individual relationships intersect and juxtapose with descriptions of intermeshed boundaries, rigid boundaries, healthy vibrant boundaries, and every other imaginable boundary identified and commented upon when it comes to dating, marriage, and so on. It is a popular topic with many book titles available. One is *Boundaries Where You End and I Begin: How to Recognize and Set Healthy Boundaries* (1998) by Ann Katherine.

The idea of boundaries is always an artificial construct serving to define and explain personal responsibilities, personal feelings, personal property, and one's physical person. Touching someone in a packed subway car would likely not be considered a violation of a boundary. Tapping one's shoulder to warn of a problem would likewise not likely be a boundary violation. Putting your arm around a date would also not likely be a boundary violation, but touching a more private part clearly would. Probably, boundary violations have not been either the same or as obvious in all cultures over all of recorded history.

Chapter 4:
Commitment

Cigna Loneliness Survey –
    May 1, 2018 - Today, global health service company Cigna (NYSE: CI) released results from a national survey exploring the impact of loneliness

in the United States. The survey, conducted in partnership with market research firm, Ipsos, revealed that most American adults are considered lonely. The evaluation of loneliness was measured by a score of 43 or higher on the UCLA Loneliness Scale, a 20-item questionnaire developed to assess subjective feelings of loneliness, as well as social isolation. The UCLA Loneliness Scale is a frequently referenced and acknowledged academic measure used to gauge loneliness.

The survey of more than 20,000 U.S. adults ages 18 years and older revealed some alarming findings:

- Nearly half of Americans report sometimes or always feeling alone (46 percent) or left out (47 percent).
- One in four Americans (27 percent) rarely or never feel as though there are people who really understand them.
- Two in five Americans sometimes or always feel that their relationships are not meaningful (43 percent) and that they are isolated from others (43 percent).
- One in five people report they rarely or never feel close to people (20 percent) or feel like there are people they can talk to (18 percent).
- Americans who live with others are less likely to be lonely (average loneliness score of 43.5) compared to those who live alone (46.4). However, this does not apply to single parents/guardians (average loneliness score of 48.2) – even though they live with children, they are more likely to be lonely.
- Only around half of Americans (53 percent) have meaningful in-person social interactions, such as having an extended conversation with a friend or spending quality time with family, on a daily basis.
- Generation Z (adults ages 18-22) is the loneliest generation and claims to be in worse health than older generations.
- Social media use alone is not a predictor of loneliness; respondents defined as very heavy users of social media have a loneliness score (43.5) that is not markedly different from the score of those who never use social media (41.7).

In *Happiness, Pleasure, and Judgment* (1995), author Allen Parducci proposes the theory that values related to happiness are relative and based on circumstances entirely private to the individual.

Albert Einstein famously gave a "tip" to a bellboy at the Hotel Tokyo in 1922 when he advised: "A calm and modest life brings more happiness than the pursuit of success combined with constant restlessness."

According to Aristotle, happiness depends on each of us. Happiness is the central purpose of human life and a goal unto itself. He postulated that virtue is achieved by maintaining a balance between two excesses.

How social influence, responsibility, and commitment coalesce in the individual is not something that has garnered much scholarly attention. Studies on social influence are most often limited to studies of leadership. Studies on responsibility are most often limited to business or social responsibility. Articles on commitment are most often limited to religious matters and marriage. How these three areas affect loneliness, creativity, and problem-solving is left to religious books, or books on spirituality and home-spun philosophy.

"Personal responsibility" was a phrase used at the United States Constitutional Convention when drafting the constitution. Winston Churchill opined further when he famously stated: "The price of greatness is responsibility."

"In dreams begins responsibility" is a quote from William Butler Yates writing in "Responsibilities" (1914).

The book of Proverbs in the Hebrew texts of the old bible detail responsibility in each chapter.

Existentialist, Jean-Paul Sartre said: "Man is nothing else but what he makes of himself." Owning yourself, and your own results is the essence of responsibility.

The leader steps forward with his or her own narrative to influence the story of the group. The leader takes responsibility for this, and may suffer the consequences. The leader cannot lead without taking a defined position that is subject to assault and criticism, as well as praise and reward.

Loneliness is the opposite of leadership. Loneliness does not afford the opportunity to influence, and does not provide the opportunity to apply inclusive principles. Loneliness is a void and to be avoided.

Responsibility requires a level of awareness and of accountability. An author who dissects this issue with an emphasis on personal responsibility is Peter Mulrany in *My Life is My Responsibility: Insights for Conscious Living* (2017).

In her book, *Responsibility and Judgment* (2003), author Hanna Arendt deals with the subject of moral responsibility, the need for humans to make reflective judgments, and the failure of moral responsibility in political action. Arendt lived through the dark times of the Hitler dictatorship witnessing its evil first hand. She pointed out how there was a lack of moral responsibility on the part of those who acceded to the horrible actions of the dictatorship. She showed how lack of real responsibility, with expedient self-preservation, leads people to be powerless in the face of moral evil and dictatorship. With responsibility comes risk. For Arendt, lack of responsibility was a root of evil. To be morally responsible, leaves one open to danger and loss while also opening the possibility to be truly good and truly principled.

Chapter 5:
Inclusion with the World

Habits –
The study of habits is at least as old as Aristotle (384-322 BCE). In his work on ethics, *Nicomachean Ethics*, Aristotle wrote of the role of habits

in human conduct saying: "Virtues are habits," and "A good life must contain habits as a part of routine."

In 1950, Dr. Maxwell Maltz first published his book *Psych-Cybernetic* (re-printed in 1989) writing about his discovery that the minimum amount of time required to change a habit was at least 21 days, and it often takes longer. Maltz's prescient thoughts foreshadowed the decades of self-help and personal development that followed.

The idea of transforming habits is an old one, but continues to be a timely topic that still attracts keen interest. In *The Power of Habit* (2014), Charles Duhigg, a New York Times business reporter, writes about current information and thinking about habits. He shows how changing habits can change lives, businesses, and even entire communities.

Habits may reflect our principles, but they are not likely to be principles that have been subjected to critical analysis or even current review. Habits build upon previous habits often without understanding why, and without conscious thought. Habits become so ingrained that they are accepted by the conscious and unconscious mind as being a part of our lives. Anything that is done over and over should be reviewed for conformance to the values and principles that we consciously seek to live by.

Intuition is defined as "insight, instinctive feeling, and understanding without conscious reasoning." Intuition is a type of knowing that does not involve much knowledge about how we know. Intuition often means getting our conscious minds out of the way so that we are able to listen to other ideas, or to catch feelings that come to you. There are techniques for emphasizing the less-than-conscious-knowing or intuitions that we all have. See: *Developing Your Intuition: 5 Simple Steps to Help You Live A More Intuitive Life* (2017) by Michael Hetherington. Being aware of yourself means being receptive to thoughts and feelings that have not been in your top-of-mind awareness. It means being open to insight that comes spontaneously and without strained thinking. It means being sensitive to when things seem out of place. It means trusting a thought or feeling that seems right even though it may be contrary in some way to what you have learned in the past.

In their best-selling book, *The Law of Attraction* (2006), Esther and Jerry Hicks set forth ideas that the authors claim came to them through a spirit named Abraham. The Hicks postulate that people do manifest both their positive and negative thoughts. The book entitled *The Secret* (2006) by Rhonda Byrne adopted the law of attraction, calling it the "secret" of the universe. *The Secret* was also a best seller and continues to be cited for the ideas first introduced by the Hicks.

Having met Esther and Jerry Hicks, I can say that they are very genuine and very engaging. Their ideas have resonated with many people, and explain how our thoughts and intentions are seminal to our actions and the results that we see around us. They believed that manifestations are effortless. Esther Hicks has written several more books on these ideas, which have become part of the "New Thought" culture. These ideas are not particularly spiritual, and they are not built upon ethics or morals nor do they suggest the importance of principles or values. Finding one's own connection to the transcendent and the infinite was not the primary goal of the Hicks' teachings.

Winston Churchill –

The life of Winston Churchill (1874-1965) is a great example of one who searched for his own principles and learned to apply them to his outer world. Churchill lived the expression attributed to Albert Einstein as interpreted by Bob Samples: "The intuitive mind is a sacred gift and the rational mind is a faithful servant. We have created a society that honors the servant and has forgotten the gift." Churchill did not receive a university education, but was self-educated. A prolific author, he is best known for being the British Prime Minister of England during the Second World War standing up to the tyranny of Adolf Hitler and marshalling the forces of the free world to soundly defeat him. Churchill's life is truly a tribute to the principled man, and a study in both how to adapt to the world and how to influence it. Many biographies have been written in tribute and analysis of Churchill's life and times. Many find his life to be both fascinating and entrancing.

Mahatma Gandhi –

Mohandas Karamchand Gandhi (1869-1948), known as Mahatma Gandhi, was an Indian born attorney in South Africa who returned to India to lead the movement to gain independence from the British Empire. Gandhi developed and implemented non-violent protest methods using them effectively to mobilize and energize the Indian people in the independence struggle. Without doubt, his ideas and his spirit have motivated a great deal of social change in the past three quarters of a century. He is most important in the study of the principled human being who carried his principles to the highest refinement. Gandhi is truly a shining example of one who lived his values in every way, and served as an example for other great and principled leaders, including Martin Luther King, Jr., Nelson Mandela, and Mother Teresa.

The idea of self-acceptance began in the twentieth century in the field of psychology. Marie Jahoda, a social psychologist and prolific author, postulated that one characteristic of a "normal" person is realistic self-esteem and acceptance. Since then, the idea of self-acceptance has evolved into a mainstay of clinical psychology and positive psychology. For these disciplines, personal change is possible only when there is acceptance of one's own abilities and limitations. Whether these methods of analyzing personal change are perfectly correct, it cannot be denied that personal change, personal growth, and personal balance require assessments that are entirely personal in nature. The problem with self-acceptance as a mantra is that we are all changing, always finding new issues, new concerns, and feelings that need to be incorporated and absorbed. If awareness of change and the need for flexibility is part of self-acceptance, then the term works. If self-awareness means finding the limited person with flaws and problems that must be accepted, the term needs a bit of re-definition. Ideas of limitation always breed limitation. Ideas of abundance and greater possibilities tend to produce abundance and new realities.

Chapter 6:
Powerful Inclusion

George Washington –
  There are many good biographies written about George Washington with two that deal in depth with the character of the man and how he became effective in his many leadership roles:
  • *Washington: A Life* (2010) by Ron Chernow
  • *George Washington: A Biography* (1994) by Washington Irving

Franklin Delano Roosevelt –
  A fabulous biography is:
  • *Franklin Delano Roosevelt: Champion of Freedom* (2003) by Conrad Black

Booker T. Washington –
  A recent influential biography is:
  • *Booker T. Washington: A Biography* (2012) by Jasmine Evans

Principles are necessary to be effective, but adaptability is known to be an integral part of responding to life changes. Resilience and the ability to respond to new challenges is a vital component to effective life responses. There are many books and papers written that research and describe these characteristics. One worth reading is called: *Resilience: The Science of Mastering Life's Greatest Challenges* (2012) by Steven Southwick and Dennis Charney

The failure of leadership has been the subject of many studies and tracts dealing with business management. History is filled with leaders who did not fulfill their tasks, who took their ideas to an extreme, and who were unable to adapt to difficult times. One such leader was Jawaharlal Nehru, the first Prime Minister of India. An interesting biography that addresses his failures is: *The God Who Failed: An assessment of Jawaharlal Nehru's Leadership* (2014) by Madhav Godbole.

Gratitude is one of the four lessons that I wrote about in my book *Turbulence in the River: Four Lessons and Two Truths.* I wrote: "Gratitude is a state of being. It is also a process. In its state of being, it has a set of attitudes that lead one to being open to as many variations and styles as possible. The state of being allows always for a sense of awe that the possibilities available from the resources of the universe are endless." Gratitude is a state of being, a state of mind, and a process of relating to all the sensory input we have. Gratitude is the first lesson and the foundation for understanding ourselves and our world. It requires an open mind, an open heart, and a willingness to learn and experience all that we reasonably can. We can't be truly grateful if we are not open to the world. Being open to the world expands our options allowing us to fully explore the excitement and wonder of experience. Gratitude also keeps us open to the process of change as we respond to the changes around us encouraging us to savor and enjoy our experiences.

Core values include among others: Love, Patience, Kindness, Forgiveness, Trust, Selflessness, Compassion, Integrity, Honesty, and Sincerity. The term "core values" is often used interchangeably with core principles. Although they are clearly bound together, core principles involve more the personal image we have of those values, and the methods we have adopted to express those values. For instance, if Kindness is one of our core values, then the principle of Kindness will also involve how we apply Kindness in our personal lives, how we want others to treat us, and how we treat others. Core values may be widely shared, but also be quite different in the principles that each individual adopts to understand and express them.

Ideals can be thought of as the purest distillation of our core values, and the best expression and the goals of our principles. For instance, the ideal of Honesty is the person who cannot tell a lie. Ideals are quite often clearly not attainable, and they serve only as goals of behavior and thought.

Chapter 7:
Self-awareness

Awareness and Self-awareness are threads that run through many spiritual and psychological practices. For instance, self-awareness is an essential part of what Eckhart Tolle wrote about in his best-selling book, *The Power of Now* (1997). Tolle's book is centered on the idea that we must be fully present in the immediate moment or the Now. That cannot be done without a fine-tuned awareness of who we are and what we are. It means bringing all the senses into the Now. Being truly present means being truly aware.

Awareness is an essential part of the practice of Buddhism. Buddhists call it self-awareness without a "self" by saying that there is no self, but only awareness. Whatever you call it – awareness or self-awareness – it means that your senses are open and that you are receiving input into what is going on in the world around you.

Being self-aware means being aware of your innermost feelings, your thoughts, and your dreams. It does not being mean being obsessive about your dreams, thoughts or feelings, but to experience complete and pure observation that allows you to be fully aware of what is around you. Complete awareness is certainly not something that can be accomplished by any known living being. Are we, for instance, seeing all that presented to our eyes, or are we seeing only what our eyes are capable of seeing? Are we hearing all the sound around us, or only what we are capable of hearing? The answer is clearly that we are limited by our senses and our mental capability of taking it in without interference by something else.

Thoughts are a practical part of our reality, and can be fleeting, intrusive and sometimes occupying all our capabilities of emotion and cognition. If you've ever been chased by a carnivorous wild animal, you know what I mean.

Anything that increases our ability to be aware of what is around us and within us helps to enhance our self-awareness. Being present, calm, non-judgmental, and sensitive increases awareness. Being sensitive to our thoughts, feelings, and dreams helps to increase our self-awareness.

Lucid Dreaming is a type of dreaming that allows the dreamer to feel consciously present in the dream. This kind of dreaming allows both a more vivid form of dreaming and the conscious ability to interact with the dream. Being aware of your dreams and being able to make sense of them is a revealing exercise in the true nature of our inner feelings and thoughts. Curiously, being able to dream lucidly is enhanced when one approaches all of life as if it is part of the dream process. A dream process is something happening to us, or that we are observing without consciously thinking it. This kind of dreaming is similar to the Buddhist way of thinking about awareness and similar to some types of meditation, which clearly requires calmness and non-judgment. If you experience lucid dreaming, find out what it is without prior judgment or over-thinking. It seems a lot like mindfulness, which is a current and well-respected way to place attention on the present moment. Mindfulness discards thoughts of the past and the future.

Savoring is an activity that emphasizes spending enough time with your sensory input to understand and appreciate it. You may decide, after you spend time savoring something, that you don't really relish it and will not seek the sensory input again. That happened with me when I ate limburger cheese. Living in the moment may be an ultimate goal, but being open to all aspects of what is happening around you must be the goal as well. That inevitably means understanding what is going on around you. It does not mean pretending that what you are seeing has no connection to the past or the future. Reality is not such, and we are not wired such, that we can concentrate only on the present moment. It cannot be disputed that we cannot plan for the future without perception of the past. We want to acquire the ability to exclude intrusive thoughts and feelings, but the very fact that we are making the attempt proves that the thoughts and feelings are strongly present within us. Intrusive feelings and intrusive thoughts can be useless and worthless or they can be important indicators of important parts of ourselves in need of attention.

Mindfulness and awareness as spiritual practices make sense because they allow us to feel the fullness of what we have learned, felt, and discovered without making judgment and without being carried away with thoughts and feelings that do not apply to the present moment. The fuller and perhaps even the crazier the life, the better the results will be when mindfulness and awareness are cultivated.

Chapter 8:
Preparing for Empowerment

Finding out who we are, what we want, and how we want to get it is an essential part of nearly all aspects of our personal, spiritual and social growth. We need to know these things about ourselves if we are to be successful in our spiritual journeys. We need them if we are to be successful in our work and in our personal relationships. We need them if we are to find balance and comfort in our lives. We need them if we are to be effective and powerful. How to achieve this process of finding out what we want and how to get it, and what is involved in the personal search for it, are the essential issues of nearly all psychological, spiritual and religious disciplines. It is at the heart of most of the New Age studies.

Studying Neuro Linguistic Programming (NLP) to a Masters level taught me a whole lot about how humans think and how we can change thoughts and feelings. NLP taught me that much of life is a process, and not fixed states of being. We speak for instance of "allergies" in the nominative sense (as if allergies are nouns, unchanging and forever), while NLP looks at allergies as processes of the immune system that can most often be altered without drugs. In NLP, I learned that many psychological and physical states can be changed if we find the origins of the situations that gave rise to them, provide resources that were missing or damaged and rebuild a state of balance and health. The NLP processes can be very effective in many situations. I witnessed and created changes myself in my training. NLP speaks of the "well-formed outcome" that is achievable if it is articulated in positive terms, identifies all necessary resources, understands the steps to be taken, and seriously considers the affect it will have on ourselves and others when the "well-formed outcome" is achieved. In my own search for personal and spiritual growth, I have grafted onto this formula the additional initial steps of searching my own internal feelings and my own heart to find out what seems to be missing and what needs to be supplemented or changed. I suggest that, without this additional step, we will not necessarily be happy when our outcome is reached. I have realized the importance of being careful, sensible, and sensitive as to what I am asking for, knowing I just might get it.

There is an old expression that "The thought is mother or father to the deed." I learned long ago that thoughts are not alone in this process. The heart, intuition, and feelings are part and parcel of the deed as well. I learned that our feelings about a thought tell us whether the thought is fully formed or missing something. In *Turbulence in the River*, I set forth a process that works to help us find out what we want by incorporating our emotions, or thoughts, and our heart spirit in that process.

Psychoanalysis showed me the importance of dreams in our ability to understand ourselves. I have learned that we never stop growing and we never fully plumb the depths of our own unconscious minds. The more we learn about ourselves, the richer our lives become.

Early in my adult life, I learned that respecting and appreciating change is important. When I was 18 years old, I began studying the *I Ching*, which taught that the process of change has familiar patterns that can be learned and used to understand and influence change in our lives. The *I Ching* taught me that inclusion, in the larger scheme of our existence, is inevitable and must be studied seriously. How we manage our own existences directly affects the changes we experience.

The *I Ching* is the oldest book of wisdom in the world. The ancient Chinese discovered a binary system constructing 8 trigrams and 64 hexagrams that continually change to create known patterns with known issues and consequences. The *I Ching* curiously mirrors the genetic code as described in Dr. Martin Schonberger fascinating book, *The I Ching and the Genetic Code: The Hidden Key to Life* (1992). Somehow the same formula and the same patterns have allowed the fantastic complexity of life on Earth, and serve to explain the complexities of human lives. We are all unique and special, yet we all share similar patterns.

Emotional development through emotional understanding is important for our own personal growth. Without it, we have great difficulty in being effective in our personal and social lives. Emotional awareness is essential to Compassion which, I learned, is essential to finding our own personal internal inclusion. Personal inclusion is a precursor to inclusion in the world. In his book, *Emotional Intelligence,* Daniel Goleman is credited with spreading the understanding of emotional intelligence. In the past, emotional intelligence was seriously underestimated. Now that emotional intelligence is being seriously studied, it is helping to show that we are all much more than just logical thought.

Chapter 9:
Shaping Your World

How is it that some people make things happen in their lives and get what they want, while others flounder getting only what the world begrudgingly gives them? How is it that some people seem to know what they want and find it, while others can't tell you what they really want? How is it that some people are able to develop personal influence in the world while others can't seem to even get people to listen to them?

The life of Walt Disney is a case study of a person who was able to push for what he really wanted, and, in doing so, truly changed not only the immediate world around him, but the world of nearly all the humans alive. Walt Disney accomplished this by identifying what he wanted early in his life. He then kept pushing his ideas until he had the entire country and even the entire world appreciating his revolutionary way of entertaining others. He did not stop with cartoons, but continued into the broader of world of filmmaking, and then created the ultimate fantasy with his amusement parks, Disneyland and Disney World. Disney's influence is more pervasive than almost any human being of the past few centuries.

Walt Disney's standards and principles are easy to find. One book I recommend is: *Walt Disney: The Triumph of the American Imagination* (2006) by Neal Gabler. Several principles guided Disney's actions: seeking what motivated and interested people; belief that he needed to work as hard as possible to achieve what he could imagine; and an insistence on perfection from others.

Walt Disney's life shows us that we don't need to be perfect people to achieve greatness. In fact, we all have flaws that others might find undesirable. In Disney's case, he pushed himself so far that he often had financial difficulties as well as mental health issues including depression. Nevertheless, Disney never let negativity interfere with his principles, and shaped the entire world by his vision and persistence. Disney is my poster child for the person who knows what he wants and will not stop until he gets it.

Chapter 10:
Gratitude

The Merriam-Webster dictionary defines gratitude as "the quality of being thankful, readiness to show appreciation for and return kindness". However gratitude is defined, it is the thoughts and the feelings that there is something we recognize that has either helped us or pleased us or added to the enjoyment and satisfaction in our lives. As part of my spiritual journey chronicled in my book, *Turbulence in the River*, I learned that the true depths of gratitude involved much more than the thoughts and feelings of appreciation. Gratitude is rooted in the full range of our experiences. Gratitude means opening up to all experience so that you can have the understanding and awareness of what has been made available for you. Therefore, the attitude of Gratitude means putting aside limited thinking and being as free of judgment as you can be. We are all involved in what I have referred to as the Realm of Gratitude. Without a dispassionate viewpoint and an expanded view of the importance of experience, appreciation is limited. We can only be thankful for something we are aware of and something we can appreciate.

Savoring has begun to attract academic attention. In his 2006 book, *Savoring: A new Model of Positive Experience*, Fred Bryant, a professor at Loyola University, explores the psychology of enjoyment explaining processes and understandings through which people are able to manage positive emotions. Along with Erica Chadwick and Katherina Kluwe, Bryant collaborated in writing an article for the *International Journal of Wellbeing*, "Understanding the processes that regulate positive emotional experience: Unsolved problems and future directions for theory and research on savoring" (2011).

In *Turbulence in the River*, I explained that savoring and excess share certain qualities: "Savoring is a simple act, requiring only that time be given both during the act of resource enjoyment and for so much time afterward as the vibration and energy of the act continues to keep the sensation of enjoyment that the act allowed." I also wrote: "When it gratifies deeply we may well try it over and over to the extent that it goes from excess to obsession and grabs us with an addiction that we are at a loss to explain." How do we separate what is simple savoring from what is excessive and obsessive? This is both a personal question as well as a question for the appropriate professional. However, from a broader perspective, we can see that both savoring and addictions deal with exploring and experiencing our outer world or what I called the "Realm of Gratitude". This realm has all we need and should have all we want. How we deal with this realm is how we develop our selves, our values, and our principles. The Realm of Gratitude is truly at the foundation of our spiritual natures and always mediates how we deal with our physical selves and our physical world.

Along with savoring, gratitude has also begun to attract academic and scientific interest. Robert Emmons, scientific expert on gratitude wrote *The Psychology of Gratitude* (2004) as well as *Gratitude Works! A 21 Day Program for Creating Emotional Prosperity* (2013). Emmons shows the theory and the evidence that being positive and thankful is something of great value.

Mitchel Adler and Nancy Fagley studied appreciation at Rutgers University producing an abstract "Appreciation: Individual Differences in Finding Value and Meaning as a Unique Predictor of Subjective Well-Being" (2005). Adler and Fagley viewed gratitude as a component of appreciation. In their study, Adler and Fagley defined appreciation as "acknowledging the value and the meaning of something, and feeling a positive connection to it." Although they analyze the subjective reaction to things, Adler and Fagley stress the experiential aspect of appreciation and the evident need to notice and acknowledge that which is being appreciated. They painstakingly set forth the various aspects of appreciation including "life satisfaction", "positive and negative affect", "emotional self-awareness", "dispositional optimism" and "spirituality". They also devised a subscale of eight aspects of appreciation: focus, awe, ritual, present moment, self/social comparison, gratitude, loss/adversity, and interpersonal. Their study, interesting and revealing, is commended for reading on the subject of appreciation and is readily available on Google. There is great usefulness in understanding appreciation because appreciating your world can help you find or strengthen the values and principles that will make you satisfied, powerful, and effective.

Chapter 11:
The Now

The River of Nows takes us beyond what others such as Eckhart Tolle, author of the acclaimed book *The Power of Now*, envisioned. The metaphor of a flowing river helps us realize that, as we encounter the Now, we must consider the current and past influences in our lives that cause turmoil. In contemplating the instant of Now, we sense that there are many instances of Now colliding like the torrent of turbulence in wild rivers. Turbulence can keep us from truly living in the instant of Now. To achieve our balanced self, we need to escape the turbulence. We do that by gaining perspective, which helps achieve calmness, and calmness allows us to open into compassion.

To achieve perspective, calmness, and compassion, one can employ various techniques and meditation practices – some simple, some more complex – and some derived from religious or spiritual traditions. No matter the method, if it brings calmness into our lives or lends itself to a more expansive and inclusive perspective, it has value. Calmness allows you to escape the emotions and thoughts that have kept you bound in the turbulence of the river.

The instant point of Now is also that point that connects with all of the infinite resources of the universe. Quantum Physics teaches that there are parallel universes and maybe infinite universes. Our conscious connections occur in the instant of Now. Our memories keep us connected to the past. Our projections of the future help us plan our lives, but also distract us from being present in the instant of Now. No one can tell you exactly how to be true to yourself, open to the future, and present for the Now. By being intuitive, conscious, aware and open, we create a life that is a perfect work of art with enough flexibility to change and grow. Be sensitive to the changes while always being true to yourself.

In *Turbulence in the River*, there are long conversations about the nature of the River of Nows. Each instant of Now partakes of the infinite universe which it expresses. Each instant is so infinitesimally short that we could never hope to capture it, but can only see the instances as they flow together. We see outlines, and often we see what we hope to find, but we miss things that are much more obvious if only we knew how to find them. Turbulence and the upset that inevitably comes along with turbulence are the biggest distractions to both perceiving and enjoying the Now. Understanding how to navigate in the Now, being always aware of who you are, will help you to find your principles and shape them to fit your needs. Once you identify your principles, you cannot expect the process to end because the river is always moving and change is always happening. Even slight changes may sooner or later put you in a vastly different place. Being aware of your surroundings and yourself prepares you to make the necessary changes to both your principles and how you present them. Principles are meant to express who you are and allow you the best interaction with your world.

Chapter 12: Congruence

If you truly want something, you should not be thinking and acting in ways that discourage that something from happening. On a first date, you should not be acting in ways that your date would find distasteful and, after you have been married for years, you should be not even be doing that at all. When you are trying to communicate something, it is not wise to do something that contradicts what you are saying. If you want something, act like you want it. If your principles are not congruent with your values, they will not serve you in either the short or long term. Your principles will also not be well received or feel comfortable if they are contradictory to the values of the group in which you might be expressing them.

The late Virginia Satir – one of the models for the theories of Neuro Linguistic Programming and world famous for her family therapy techniques – made a substantial point of the issue of congruent behavior. Satir believed that conflicts and difficulties in families often arise from members not expressing their deepest feelings. She found this to be the basis for much misunderstanding pointing out that incongruent behavior is often due to action from the unconscious and not from purposeful action. Interesting conversations with Satir have been recorded by Dr. Jeffrey Mishlove in *Thinking Allowed, Conversations on the leading Edge of Knowledge and Discovery* (1995). Satir believed that the origin of communication came from different places within each human being. She stressed that people frequently avoid communicating their "vulnerable" sides for fear of being embarrassed or hurt. She does not say that it will always be easy to say what we mean, but she does say that we will never reach a truly functional and happy relationship unless we do that. Satir is quoted as saying: "The ones who really are willing to stick their necks out and to say 'this is what I believe', and at the same time are not putting other people down, will eventually rise to the top." By saying this, she confirms that heartfelt principles called into action create power, but without congruent thinking, emotion, and unconscious action nothing can be achieved.

Virginia Satir also said: "Self-esteem for me is the willingness to say where you are." She said that we have to be free to "rock the boat". In her own way, Satir is saying that we all must be allowed to speak and act our true principles, even if they may not be readily appreciated.

To be truly powerful in a way that is sustainable and without experiencing a punishing reaction means to not only get what you want, but to do so in a way that is aware of the consequences of your actions. This is where the teachings of karma can be of assistance.

There are twelve laws of karma. See: *Karma and Happiness: The 12 laws of Karma That Will Change Your Life* (2017) by Jonathan Reid.

1. The Great Law: There is cause and effect to your actions; what you sow is what you reap. What you put out there is what you get back.
2. The Law of Creation: What you allow yourself to be, you will likely be. You have no choice but to be yourself. You get to decide what that is. Life does not happen by itself; surround yourself with what you want. If it is not something you want, then don't put it around yourself.
3. The Law of Humility. What you resist persists in your life. You may not have all the answers. If it is opposition, let it be, don't resist. Rather go into your own internal space and let yourself be what you are, separate and apart from that which you are finding in opposition. If your principles are not being received, don't use a hammer to make others accept them, take them inside and let them feed you. Be ready to accept that, perhaps, they do not work as you had hoped. Be humble. Humility will help you find the principles that work. Powerful principles do not necessarily mean that you lord them over others, but rather that they are being accepted for what they are. The Law of Humility requires that you always ask what is right, not just what is powerful.
4. The Law of Growth cryptically states: "wherever you are, there you are." Changes in who you are change those around you. Seeking your true self will allow the world around you to change.
5. The Law of Responsibility. What you see around you is a mirror of what you have inside. You are responsible for your path in life.
6. The Law of Connection. Every step in your life is connected. Your future is connected to your desires. See how the dots are

connected, and if it does not come to you, ask your unconscious to reveal or express it to you.

7. The Law of Focus. We move in the direction on which we focus. Limited thinking causes a person to take limited action. Limited action leads to more limited action. Focusing means paying attention to what you want, and also to what the consequences will be. It really means being aware of what you want and why you want it.

8. The Law of Giving and Hospitality. If you believe something is good, then give it. Be hospitable to what it attracts. If it is worth giving, it is worth getting in return. If you cannot give and be hospitable at the same time, then you don't give at all. In terms of principles: if the principles you act upon are good, give them freely, and expect them to be returned on you. If you are dubious about the effect on you, don't act on them with others.

9. The Law of Here and Now. What you get in life happens right now, not last year or next year. Being as much as you can be right now brings you the most you can get right now.

10. The Law of Change. You have an obligation to gain as much perspective and be as objective as possible about yourself. Change will come about in your internal life, in how others see you, and how you are rewarded or punished only when you yourself decide to make the changes.

11. The Law of Patience. For a farmer, patience is doing what is necessary to grow crops, waiting for the harvest, and then spending the time to complete the harvest. Patience means applying yourself to what you want, then giving it the necessary time to manifest.

12. The Law of Significance and Inspiration. What you get is what you give. If you are positive, what you get back will likely be positive. If it is negative, or received as negative, perhaps the significance is not there, and perhaps it is not inspirational to others. Once something achieves significance and there is inspiration, then we see the application of the principle that the

whole is greater than the sum of its parts. Something new has been created. Power comes most effectively when principles are applied that are calculated to be significant and provide inspiration. A simpler way to say this: If it falls flat, try something else.

The reason to focus on karma is to emphasize that we all have an obligation to be aware of our principles, how best we can apply them, how they are received, how we can review them and how we need to change them if they are not working for ourselves or for others. To be truly and properly congruent means that your inner self, your values and your principles must congruently serve what you are doing and who you are doing them with. Only you can judge whether that is happening.

Chapter 13:
Turmoil

In *Alchemy of the Heart: Transform Turmoil into Peace through Emotional Integration* (2008), author Michael Brown stresses unconditional self-perception writing that peace happens only when we choose to get better at feeling.

Byron Wesley has written an impactful small book, *The Power of Adversity* (2017), exploring the skills that people can use to overcome adversity including meditation and connecting to the subconscious mind. His book is one of a great many written over millennia that have dealt with the issue of overcoming adversity. The Greek philosopher Herodotus taught that adversity was a teacher.

In *Turbulence in the River*, I dealt with turmoil as an inevitable part of every personal and interpersonal conflict. I explored turmoil as an inevitability in every life due to both the complexity of each moment of the Now and the fact that there are always competing interests that intersect in every life. I discussed that it is essential to learn the skills of calmness and compassion in order to move beyond the turbulence and towards the internal incorporation of all the parts of one's self. If we are aware and pay attention, turbulence will reveal what we need to find within ourselves to build a full and balanced self.

Understanding the role that turbulence plays is important in learning the skills necessary to examine our principles and how they are being expressed. When there is a conflict in the expression of our principles, we can be sure that there is an issue of turmoil and turbulence. We have a chance of self-examination when we calmly and compassionately explore how this relates to our inner self. We may stick with our principles, and we often should, but self-examination is important both for reinforcing our principles and, possibly, for discovering unknown inner needs or issues.

Chapter 14:
Integrity

Most of the literary works on the issue of integrity focus on standing on moral principles and ethics that are often strict and inflexible. Some authors write about standing firm in your word. Others write about doing the "right thing". Such books are easily found using a quick Google search.

Integrity, along with everything else in life, is something that looks and feels different depending on the situation in which it is being viewed. Ultimately, you have to be the judge of your own integrity because everyone has multiple sides, multiple parts, and different agendas depending on circumstances and on the times. You will know whether contradictions inherently make sense due to changing agendas, needs of the world with which you are interacting, changes in your own view of yourself and world, and so on. If others are noting a lack of integrity, perhaps it is time to do an inventory of your own needs and goals, as well as your own sense of balance. What others think about you is not the deciding judgment. Only you can make that judgment. Integrity means integrating and accepting yourself.

Chapter 15:
Exclusionary Thinking

Exclusionary thinking is best exemplified in tribalism, racism, and among many religious groups. All justify the exclusion of outsiders in order to maintain the security and identity of the group. Politics in the United States has taken on heavy attributes of tribalism. One is either in or out of the group with outsiders usually demeaned and shunned. In *Moral Tribes: Emotion, Reason, and the Gap Between Us and Them* (2013), author Joshua Greene writes that: "human brains were designed for tribal life with an 'us v. them' mentality." Greene, a Harvard Professor and faculty member of the Center for Brain Science, says that the modern world has "shrunk" and the lines that divide people now have become hardened moral judgments often based on false beliefs. Greene suggests that "moral judgments" are determined by two competing processes: emotional (less controlled and more automatic) and controlled, conscious reasoning.

The problem with the "us v. them" mentality is that there will always be others outside your current circle, your city, your country, etc. The question is how much you prize your own development, and how much you prize the growth of that development interacting with others. We know that stunting your own inner world also stunts your ability to interact with the world. We also know that stunting the outer world does not allow the inner world to grow and to develop. We should, therefore, be suspicious of thinking that describes limitations of both inner growth and inclusionary actions. The two are inextricably linked. For principles to be dynamic and successful, they must be formulated and calibrated to include as much of the visible and present world as is reasonably possible.

Tribalism allows justification for acts of expediency. The principles of the tribe are dictated by the tribe for the preservation of the tribe by using emotional arguments and circular thinking fallacies. Inasmuch as the tribe is exclusive, any who live outside the tribe tend to be identified as antagonistic. This further justifies the tribe.

Racism divides people into groups based on nothing more than appearance. It is the ultimate invidious discrimination because it allows inclusion based only on appearance and demands exclusion based only on appearance too. The mere act of exclusion is used to justify itself. As with nearly all blanket exclusions, it is lacking in true bona fides. Yet in its many forms, racism is a main driver of exclusion and vicious discrimination in the world.

Chapter 16:
Success and Direction

People pay a lot of money for personal coaching for their personal and professional lives. If you can afford it and you prefer a structured view of your goals, actions, or your methods of interaction with others, then it may be of benefit to have the perspective and the direction of another. However, most folks can neither afford personal coaching nor do they have the time to take part in it. Furthermore, you cannot ask someone other than yourself what you want or what is right for you. They will never know, because only you can know. The search for what you want is always an inner search. Perhaps others can help guide you on your inner search, but until you have gained inner access to your intuition, your heart, and to the quiet part of your mind, it is not likely that you will find something that truly resonates.

You can always ask others how you appear to them. You can ask them if your requests make sense or are burdensome or offensive. But if you ask what questions you are supposed to ask, then you probably have not given any thought to the subject at hand. Success is always personal and relative to given situations. Direction is important because we assume that there is movement going somewhere. For those who are highly ambitious, success may be achieved more often than for those with less ambition. Ambition means that you are striving. Too much ambition may tax you unduly or put you in situations that you are not prepared to experience. Not enough ambition will mean you are not really looking for what may help you grow and develop. Not everyone feels the need to grow and develop. Some people are content to sit and let things happen to them.

No one has the right to question your ambition, your definition of success, or the direction that you choose. Well-meaning advice may sometimes derail you from the proper direction. Nothing is fool-proof and every action has consequences, but how you judge your own success and the direction you take during your life is your own business. You can adopt someone else's definitions and head in their direction, but unless you internalize that direction and make it your own, you risk finding yourself in a place that you did not seek and living your life by someone else's dreams.

Everyone is going to find a time when they realize that they need to change some or many things in their life. This realization may come over time, or it may come overnight. When that happens, we must seek ways to redefine success for ourselves and we must explore other directions. When that happens, we must ask the questions again of what we want, how we can get it, who will be affected by it, and what will happen to us if we get it. Everything in life has risk, and nothing is perfect. If you make the decision that there is something you need, then you must go for it or do without. There is an old expression that he or she who hesitates is lost. The examined life, lived with awareness, acting as kindly as possible, and willing to take responsibility, usually has the advantage to make the best decisions on what principles to use and how to use them. If you act on those principles, you should never have to apologize for your actions. The old expression "you should stand on your principles" means that you have to make sure that your principles can carry your weight.

Chapter 17:
Existential Crises at the Crossroads of Life on Earth

An existential crisis is something that affects, or at least seems to affect, one's very existence threatening the very basis of who and what we are. It means that something is wrong and needs to be changed. An unfortunate reaction of many people to an existential crisis is that they isolate and protect themselves, thinking either that scarcity is the cause of the problem, or that an external threat is to blame. Most do not look inward to see what principles are being applied and even fewer wonder how their own thoughts and behavior might change things. It is rare that people want to take any personal responsibility for problems they think are remotely external to themselves. Also, there seems to be a disconnect between what people objectively believe will happen, and how they feel they should either become involved or lend their voices to a discussion of the matter. People will say "It is beyond me" when they feel either powerless or removed to the point of being ineffective. People will pass by a fire, or someone who has fallen, and lend no help. It is not clear whether people's lives are more insular, more self-absorbed, or just powerless, but until it happens in their own backyard, most folks won't get involved.

If you want to be a person of powerful principles, and you want to use them for others and for your own benefit, then you have a personal duty to be aware of what is affecting or will affect your life. Your awareness may lead to some action, or perhaps a discussion to bring awareness to others. When it comes to the issue of helping others, there is no better story than the one about the good Samaritan found in the Gospel of

Luke. This story describes personal inclusion in the affairs of a stranger. Samaritans were not Jews, and so the Samaritan could have ignored the half-dead and beaten stranger, just as a priest and another prominent Jewish person did. Why would the Samaritan treat the beaten man as he would have done for one of his own tribe or his own home? What did he get out of it? It seems inescapable that the Samaritan did so because his best principles of inclusion required him to do so irrespective of gain or reward. His actions were inclusion at the most self-less level. The reward was simply that which comes from inclusion without desire for gain or advancement. The most reasonably inclusive behavior is always the preferred behavior. Exclusive behavior does not bring the same rewards. In the bible story, the good Samaritan did not help the stranger in order to gain eternal rewards, he simply did it because his principles of inclusion with humanity required it. That is the same attitude that must motivate all who are interested in confronting the existential crises of our day. When you use your best principles that connect you to the myriad parts of yourself, and when you realize that the best parts of yourself are confirmed and enhanced by inclusion with others, you will have no choice other than to lend a hand, or whatever you have, when you encounter someone in need of rescue. This better aspect of humanity is essential to our basic humanity. There is a profound duty of kindness and responsibility for us, for the groups we join with, the countries we inhabit, and the great world in which we live. Few of us are always kind even to ourselves. Most of us have some element of irresponsibility in the present day or have had in the past. To the extent that the principles we use interacting with the world do not allow us to maximally incorporate kindness and responsibility, the effectiveness of our principles of inclusion are minimized. We are not talking about short term reward or win-lose propositions, but instead about ways that effectively expand the human capability of responding to crises that affect our existence. Everyone has heard of the stories of a person, sometimes a child, or sometimes an animal stuck down a well or some other place of extreme danger. The collective actions of rescue show the best aspects of dedicated inclusion.

Made in the USA
Monee, IL
22 January 2020